LEADING WITH INTEGRITY

Build Your Capacity
for Success and Happiness

George B. Brunt

Edited by Georgia B. Davis

LUNAR PUBLISHING

Manufactured in the United States of America

10 9 8 7 6 5 4 3 2 1

ISBN # 978-0-9838181-5-1

TABLE OF CONTENTS

FOREWORD

In my book, I share a philosophy called *visionary leadership*. People believe that if they are visionaries, they will have lots of friends and supporters, but often that is not the case. Being a visionary leader can be lonely, and it also makes you a target. In his book, *Leading With Integrity—Build Your Capacity for Success and Happiness*, George Brunt radically suggests that the reader takes the road less traveled and become a target by standing strong and tall above the norm. The required work toward integral leadership is a lifelong commitment—you will never master it and you will never graduate from being a student of this curriculum. I applaud George for his courageous message.

– Winn Claybaugh
Dean and Cofounder of Paul Mitchell Schools
Author of *Be Nice (Or Else!)*

PREFACE

This book has been largely influenced by two very prominent people in my life.

First, my wife, Leslie, has been my most important mentor and counselor. She has a keen intellect and an uncanny way of sorting out complexities into clarity. Her ability to kindly and directly confront me with the truth has shaped both my writing and my life, as it has the lives of our children. Despite her awareness of correct principles, she consistently displays patience to allow me to come to my own understanding.

When our children were very young, I marveled at how she reasoned with them. She taught me—as I observed her teaching them—that every action has a consequence. She made no attempt to scold or diminish them. Instead, she held up the standard of correct principles, teaching them they were always free to choose their actions, but they were not free to choose the consequences of their actions. Our children have heeded these lessons, and have grown to become men and women of enormous capacity and talent. They, too, have become my mentors. It is this simple observation that has inspired me to focus on the interaction among law, actions, and results.

Second, I was fortunate in my undergraduate studies to have studied under Stephen R. Covey when he was a professor at Brigham Young University. He challenged the way I saw the world and made a clear connection in my mind between the thoughts and actions we habitually choose to take and the results we achieve in our lives. Each year we try to reconnect with each other with our wives for an afternoon or evening. I have been able to observe the master teacher in home settings. He is truly a man who walks his talk, and it has indeed produced the results in his life that he predicted many years ago.   During one of these reconnection visits, we were discussing why people do not habitually act in accordance with principles they know to be true. Stephen encouraged me to write a book on the subject. I have been working on the book for the past eight years and it has been the joy that he predicted it would be. I hope you find value in its pages. As the author, I have benefited greatly from the process and application of these principles. As with all teaching, the teacher is often the one who benefits the most.

There are many more people to thank for their contributions and efforts in connection with the book. My sister, Georgia Davis, has been instrumental in encouraging me and editing throughout the process. Steve Albrecht gave me valuable insights into the process that corrupts integrity in the corporate and individual setting. David Parker provided insights and illustrative concepts that help tell the story. Ethan Willis and Randy Garn, authors in their own right, have provided encouragement and insight into the connection between actions and their results. Winn Claybaugh agreed to be interviewed and illustrated what it takes to exercise will and take action to overcome fear and inertia. In some way, all of my family, friends, and business associates have, by their conversation and example, taught and mentored me. I will forever be indebted to all of them.

I was very fortunate to have parents who led with integrity. George Earl and Thelma Brunt instilled in me, both by their example and by their teaching, that every system has a law and obedience to the law defines the results we ultimately achieve. This book is dedicated to the lasting legacy of truth they left behind.

CHAPTER 1

THE NEED

Both personal
and corporate capacity
are directly related
to integrity.

Capacity is born out of integrity, and integrity is born of actions. A leader inspires others to go beyond thoughts and fears and take action. Some leaders get people to take actions that diminish capacity. They lead them down blind alleys into addictions and slavery. Great leaders get people to take actions that increase their capacity, that lift them to higher levels, and to a higher standard. A leader with integrity will inspire others by example and doctrine in a way that will increase their capacity to learn, love, live, and leave a meaningful legacy.

As society has developed technology and advanced in all forms of science and understanding, it has created a greater number of things to do.   This is true on the national level, and it is true on the individual level. Each new invention of the modern age should create more leisure time, yet the opposite has happened!

Years ago, as an account executive at McDonnell Douglas, a major multi-national aerospace company now a part of Boeing, I had the luxury of dictating memos to a pool of three secretaries, who in turn,would type them on typewriters. Gradually, with the advancement of word processing technologies, the era of the stenographer secretary has vanished. Now, most of us type our own memos, emails, and contracts. In addition, the expectation is higher. Most people expect a 24-hour, if not sooner, turnaround. Before, when there were three secretaries to do this same work on typewriters, nobody expected a contract to be completed in less than a week. Today people are doing more tasks more efficiently with the advent of technology, but there is definitely a lot more to do.

This transfers into all areas of life. The life of a full-time mother has been equally filled with additional tasks. Now she can chauffeur her children to continuous activities and events, shop online or in the malls, respond to and send emails from home or phone, prepare more meals on demand to accommodate her family's schedules and utilize the latest in technology to clean—continuously, if desired. There was a day, less than fifty years ago, when the life of a mother was very different. There were simply fewer options. Modern conveniences have allowed us to do more, yet they have not delivered on that elusive life of leisure.

Wouldn't it be great to have increased personal capacity, or the ability to do all that needs to be accomplished, especially the important things?

With so many demands on our time, it is not uncommon that the more important things are left undone. Myriad needs, unlimited wants, and too many options compete with our limited capacity to do everything we desire. Many of the actions we take do not support the achievement of our goals and dreams.

There is a lot of wasted motion and misdirection. People, governments, and organizations waste efforts on systems that are flawed or by taking actions that do not result in what they want, and therefore have limited capacity to achieve productive goals.

Even with the dilemma of not being able to accomplish all we wish, there has never been a better time to pursue our dreams. With the demise of the dark ages, people entered a period of renaissance, a time when people began to notice the world around them, to pursue their curiosities, and to discover new possibilities. Industry and technology have amplified this enlightenment a thousand times. Today's Renaissance man or woman has vast and varied interests to explore. It is the age of enlightenment. People throughout the world carry the Internet with them, a virtual world of discovery. You have opportunity to do so much more than your parents or grandparents could do. You have opportunity to know much more than your parents or grandparents could know. You have a greater access to obtain true knowledge in so many areas of pursuit. Our parents' generation may be known as the "greatest" generation, but our generation has the opportunity to build on the foundations they laid. You have the opportunity to be much more than your parents or grandparents could have been.

The challenge comes in living life with purpose. Leonardo Da Vinci had few of the advantages that we enjoy in our age; however he was a man of great capacity because he followed systems.[1] Men and women in our age of enlightenment should far outpace those giants of the Renaissance. It will require increased capacity in order to harness and apply this opportunity! Think of what is available to you that was not available or at least not readily available to your ancestors. Some of the things that come to mind are:

---

[1] How to Think Like Leonardo Da Vince: Seven Steps to Genius Every Day by Michael Gelb

- Today we can learn more languages with more resources.
- We can communicate more often to more people instantaneously over the Internet.
- We can quickly travel to many more places for business or pleasure.
- We can become an expert in many fields of science or discovery.
- We can have instant political influence and change lives.
- We can write and publish our own music, books, or movies, etc.

What holds us back?

All around us we see examples of world leaders who lack personal morality and try to maintain their power through compulsory means. Some company executives and politicians serve selfish interests to the detriment of their investors or constituents. There are creative people sacrificing standards of truth for shock value, students willing to cheat their way through school, lawyers milking the system for personal gain, politicians who will say whatever it takes to get elected with little follow-through, and others willing to compromise their values in order to be accepted—all with the ultimate result of failure. Could it be that we should pay greater attention to time-tested wisdom, together with the examples of prior generations? We could build on our incredible legacy and avoid the pitfalls by adhering to a higher standard of integrity.

There was a time when integrity was the ideal. Today it is rarely held up as the standard. What happened? How can the depth and breadth of technical education increase so dramatically, only to watch the personal integrity of many people, organizations, and nations sink to or remain at such deep depths? Where are our leaders and role models? Have we lost sight of what integrity is and what it can do for us as individuals, organizations, and nations?

Integrity is the key.

For reasons discussed later in this book, it is clear that no nation, corporation, or individual can reach their full potential without integrity. Integrity involves decisions each one of us makes every moment we live. It can be defined as consistent compliance with principles we know to be right. The cumulative impact of our decisions regarding integrity affects the quality of our nations, organizations, families, and personal lives.

Integrity is the key to achieving increased capacity. The more we integrate principles that produce positive consequences into our lives and organizations, the more our capacity will increase.

What is capacity and why would we want to pursue it? Capacity is the facility or power to produce, perform, or deploy. Personal capacity is the sum of an individual's mental, emotional, spiritual, and physical ability or the potential for solving problems, discovering, treating, acting, experiencing, loving, and appreciating. The greater our capacity, the more power we will have.

You have probably heard it said, "If you want something done, give it to the busiest person you know." That is true. Busy people usually accomplish their assignments because they have developed more capacity than others. This capacity has been increased by acting in a way that is consistent with correct beliefs. They avoid the failure, grief, and guilt they could experience if their actions and accomplishments were not consistent with correct beliefs.

We have become an educated, but not wise, society with unlimited access to information. We have become so tolerant of the idea everybody is right and nobody is wrong that we have lost our capacities in major ways. Our intellectualization of right and wrong has completely blurred the lines that define these concepts, and has created a society of relativity connected to desire, instead of truth. When we step back and seek perspective, we have to admit that right and wrong exist at several levels. It is not complicated. At its base level, what is right is determined by whether or not the action taken results in the hoped-for consequence. We may ask, "Did I follow the right directions to get to the place I wanted to go? Have I followed the right formula to get the result I was looking for?"

Things go wrong when actions do not yield the anticipated result. In saying this we are not talking about the concepts of good and evil. Whether you hope for a good consequence or an evil consequence, you still must take the right actions that will result in the hoped-for consequence. The difference between good and evil is determined by the quality of what you hope for. Hoping for good consequences will increase capacity if the right actions are taken to achieve those good results.

Some people have tremendous capacity to perform and always seem to do the right things that achieve the intended result; others do not.

We will make a case, in this book, that integrity, or consistently doing the right thing, results in consequences that make all the difference. Principles based on integrity that teach us how to reach a series of good results are correct principles.

As individuals, our ability to consistently apply correct principles in the technology and physical realms has far outpaced our ability to do so in the social, moral, and emotional realms. In fact, we go through continuing cycles of advance and decline in the social, moral, and emotional areas. With the rapid and continual advances in modern technology and the easy accessibility of information, we should be making the greatest progress in the history of our world regarding building individual character—or the ability to consistently do the right thing. The successes and mistakes of the past are instantly accessible to our view. Religious and self-help gurus are everywhere, yet we are in a moral and social decline, because to some people, the right thing is evil, demonstrating the inverse meaning of integrity.

Wars continue to threaten. Studies show an alarming increase of cheating in the family, school, and the workplace. Many use the enhanced accessibility of information to violate their own personal standards of decency and become chained to pornography, drugs, or other obsessions. How many men and women are there in our society who hold high moral standards in public, decrying the degeneration of our society, but browse pornography in private or abuse themselves with drugs or alcohol? One of the very means of technical improvement, the home computer, can become the facilitator of incongruence and a corresponding decline in integrity depending on how we use it and related technologies. What is actually causing this decline?

Where does it lead?   What do individuals and societies forfeit when they lose integrity?

Fossil fuels, so abundant today, will be used up in a hundred and fifty years.[2] We can survive as a society without fossil fuels; surely we will innovate and find other methods to power our cars and factories. On the other hand, we could be left powerless and in a far worse state then merely lacking fossil fuels. The basic abilities of individuals or nations to innovate and perform efficiently grind to a sudden halt when people lose integrity and begin taking actions that do not result in the hoped-for consequence. They end up on a dead end street.

Both history and current affairs are replete with examples. Low integrity is the main reason why many third-world countries cannot feed their populace and lift their nations out of poverty. Any great nation fails when it ceases to act in truth and in accordance with correct principles. Many of our great nations are headed in that direction.

When integrity fails, capacity crumbles. Consider the case of any management that starts to manipulate the financial statements, or lie, cheat, or steal. They become less productive, because they have to focus on how to conceal their dishonest actions. In the end, hiding the fraud consumes more time and effort than making productive decisions. In one case, the perpetrators met almost daily to determine how to hide the fraud from investors, auditors, bankers, lawyers, employees, and others.

Mark Twain once said, "I always tell the truth because it is too hard to remember the lies."

The same is true in our individual lives. Once we lose integrity, the guilt feelings we have, together with the actions we must take to conceal our lack of integrity, significantly reduce our productive capacity. More importantly, we can

---

[2] The Hubert Peak for World Oil theory, see www.oilcrisis.com

never get the results we want without following the rules that pertain to achieving those results. A lack of integrity just won't work in achieving our goals. It is contrary to natural law and reason.

Sincere belief is not enough. You must have the facts and take the actions that will achieve the results you desire. If you are deceived, especially with self-deception, as to what actions to take to achieve a result, you will not achieve the desired result. However, all actions have results. You will always get a result, but it may be far from the result you hoped to achieve.

Do you recall a man by the name of Jim Jones? Jim Jones began an independent ministry in Indianapolis in 1953 where he had a following of over 900 members. He was ordained eleven years later as a minister of the Disciples of Christ. In the late 60's and early 70's he moved his congregation to California, establishing two churches there called The People's Temple–the main one in San Francisco and a second in Los Angeles. His California church's membership grew to over 8,000 members. He became a community activist in San Francisco and contributed both cash and volunteers supporting various political causes. Negative press reports started to surface about Jim Jones, and in response, he moved with many of his followers to British Guyana, Africa. There, he and about 1,000 followers set up an isolated settlement later referred to as Jonestown. Jones preached the imminent end of the world as a result of nuclear war, and became increasingly paranoid. Family members of many of his followers were concerned about their loved ones as there were reports of illness, harsh and demanding work, and unacceptable living conditions. Their pleas for intervention prompted Leo J. Ryan, a congressman from California, to investigate. With permission from Jim Jones, Ryan came to visit the group's compound on November 17, 1978.

He found conditions to be as reported; in addition, there were heavily-armed guards throughout the compound. While there, several followers passed notes for help in escaping with the congressman's party. By helping these individuals find freedom, Congressman Ryan lost his own life, along with four others (three were members of the press and the fourth was a Jonestown member seeking escape). Jim Jones had panicked and sent cult guards to stop them, who started shooting at the airstrip as Ryan's group, along with some of the People's Temple members, were preparing to leave. Five were killed and eleven more wounded. Others of the party escaped into the jungle.

Realizing this would be the end of his ministry and facing retribution, Jim Jones ordered the State of Emergency, a carefully-rehearsed mass suicide drill. Every member, save for the few who escaped into the jungle, including more than two hundred eighty children, either committed suicide or was murdered that day. Nine hundred fourteen people died.

Jones' followers were sincere in their beliefs, but that is not enough. He led them to take actions that resulted in diminished capacity, and ultimately death. We must sort out the facts … what actions will truly achieve the results you are looking for? The whole Jonestown story is one of denying and running from reality. People of integrity look at real cause and effect situations; they deal with the laws that govern outcome. The Jonestown members were reduced in their choices (capacity) until they had no personal capacity left. There was no integrity in their system. It was not based on principles and laws that have been proven to work.

Our society consistently relies on integrity. As an example, every day millions climb into their automobiles and drive down paved roads. In the middle of each road is a dividing line consisting merely of yellow or white paint. Sometimes we travel along at a relatively fast pace. We might pass a thousand other cars on our journey, each car driven by a fellow citizen. This highway system is based on integrity. It simply would not work without a set of laws that govern everyone's driving. There is no freedom where there is no law, but even more than that is involved. The highway system would not work without the architects who planned and the construction workers who actually took action to build the roadway. It would not work without the taxpayers who provided the funding, the planners who devised the plan to divide the road with a painted line, and the painters who painted the lines. Even with all this foundation and infrastructure, the system still would not work if we could not rely on the integrity of the drivers coming in the opposite direction. There has to be more than law; there needs to be an ingrained, self-regulation of the law in order to achieve the desired result. There must be a high degree of assurance that the oncoming traffic is going to stay in its lane. Our very lives depend upon the fact that those oncoming drivers have brought the principles that govern this complex system into their very being. They must have integrated the system, infrastructure, and laws into their behavior.

When someone willfully violates the rules and operates a vehicle under the influence of mind-altering substances or with a reckless disregard of the rules, they often wreak disastrous consequences, both personally and in the lives of many other innocent victims. A breach of the rules is involved in the vast majority of accidents. Often it involves drinking beyond the legal limits or a disregard of the driving rules, including the speed limits or even self-absorption such as texting. Integration of the rules of driving is critical for our system to work.

As a society, we have developed drivers' education programs, testing, and licensing systems to verify that integration has been accomplished. We do not just "expect" people to comply; we "inspect" that they do so. The proper functioning of our very productive society depends on it. Our highway systems are but one example of the way integrity is the *sine que non* (essential element) of capacity.

We depend upon the majority of people in our society to integrate several key principles. Merely knowing something is not enough! It is how well we integrate those correct principles that results in increased capacity. In referring to correct principles, we are talking about truth! We are talking about the rules that govern systems. We are talking about principles that make systems work and that have a demonstrated positive effect as practiced over the ages. We are talking about what really is. The following virtues (although not a complete list) are examples of a few principles which are almost universally accepted as correct social principles:

Accountability	*Willingness to account for one's actions*
Benevolence	*Disposition to do good*
Chastity	*Pure in conduct and intention*
Commitment	*Carrying out of purpose*
Compassion	*Awareness of others' distress and a desire to lighten it*
Cooperation	*To associate with others with a common goal or for mutual benefit*
Courtesy	*Considerate behavior toward others*
Dependability	*Worthy of trust*
Diligence	*Conscientiousness in giving proper attention to a task*
Discipline	*Well-behaved and under control of oneself*
Excellence	*Seeking good qualities in high degree*

Faithfulness	*Steadfast in allegiance and loyalty*
Focus	*Concentrated awareness and effort*
Forgiveness	*Ability to not be angry or bitter toward others' offenses*
Gratitude	*Being thankful*
Honesty	*Truthful and sincere*
Humility	*A lack of false pride*
Impartiality	*Disposition to weigh both sides with fairness*
Integrity	*Honest and complete incorporation of correct principles to achieve worthwhile goals*
Kindness	*Friendly and well-meaning*
Patience	*Ability to endure delay, trouble, pain, or hardship*
Prudence	*Careful in conduct and planning ahead*
Service	*Work done to benefit another*
Temperance	*Moderation and self-restraint*

Each of these principles is achieved only through an action. Experience has confirmed to us that our actions can bring good results in our personal lives and in organizations. The ability to integrate principles is important to the individual in the same way it is important to society. We can develop greater individual capacity by integrating correct principles and the systems they govern into our individual lives. All correct principles, whether they govern organizations, transportation systems, learning systems, judicial systems, home management systems, or individuals can be stated as rules. The rules tell us what should happen in order for the system to function.

Often young people fight against the rules until they understand that rules are merely statements of how to achieve a particular result. Game playing is a critical component of growing up. By playing games, we begin to realize how important the rules are to achieving the result. Playing by the rules does not seem to come naturally. Even in games, it takes time for children to learn the value of playing by the rules. Once understood, most children become very strong advocates of playing the game by the rules. When we don't play by the rules, the whole game breaks down and there is no longer any capacity to achieve the result or even to play the game. Whenever we know for ourselves what we should do, and fail to do it, our capacity similarly decreases.

When we discover systems, learn principles that govern systems, and integrate these principles into our actions (or in other words, learn and follow the rules), our personal capacity increases. When we learn principles that govern systems, and do not integrate them into our actions, our capacity diminishes. It is, perhaps, easier for us to understand how *not* implementing the correct principles diminishes our capacity. One might argue that we may not get the result if we do not act in accordance with correct principles, but we still have the capacity. This is not true.

> ***Capacity will diminish***
> ***because we will change our beliefs***
> ***about the principles we know to be correct.***

There is a basic human trait that compels us to rationalize knowledge and behavior. When they are out of line, we must either change our beliefs or change our behavior. There is no standing idle. We are always either adjusting our standards to conform to our behavior, or we are adjusting our behavior to conform to our standards.

Most people would agree they should be honest. At the most basic level, honesty is a principle that we come to understand as children. Even though we knew that the principle was correct, how many of us attempted to get around the principle? And what was the result? We were scolded, spanked, grounded, or assigned extra chores . . . if we were lucky. The unlucky among us were not instructed by parents, and therefore had to learn firsthand the inevitable consequences of dishonesty.

The problem with dishonesty is that we know when we are being dishonest, since we can never really lie to ourselves. It was Tom Sawyer's character who said, "You can't pray (live) a lie." Since humans cannot bear incongruence, they learn to rationalize or self-justify allowing self-deceit. At some basic level, we know we are deceiving ourselves, and do it anyway. Soon there is a rationale for our behavior that allows us to repeat and continue in our errant actions, even though the actions will never result in the desired consequences. The rationalizations of dishonesty blind people to the reality they face. In the end, it will be their false beliefs about reality that will cripple their capacity.

Anyone who has reasonable life experience has witnessed this phenomenon. One of the people who was interviewed and contributed greatly to this book, William Steve Albrecht, was an expert witness for the government in a major criminal fraud case. The perpetrator, who had been a very successful businessman, and one with whom everyone was eager to do business, started making ethical compromises in his actions. He gradually lowered his standards to allow for these compromises. These small, seemingly unimportant, unethical decisions led to bigger and bigger rationalizations and ethical violations. Soon he was committing massive fraud while still believing he was acting appropriately in accordance with his standards. The problem was that he had substantially lowered his standards. This led to him being tried criminally and convicted of fraud. He served a prison sentence for his rationalizations.

Consider the case of a father who neglects spending time with his family. While he may rationalize that he is busy earning money for the family or working hard for the good of his children's future, in the end he may become an ineffective parent. Little rationalizations become bigger and bigger. Unfortunately, we can blind ourselves to reality.

Phillip Calvin McGraw, known as Dr. Phil, has featured several guests on his television program where the audience could easily identify the truth, yet the guest was clueless to his situation because of his rationalizations. The guest had lowered his or her standards to such a low level that he or she could not identify the wrongful conduct without serious intervention.

Think about how cheating on a test will limit the capacity of the person who does not learn the lesson upon which the test is based. What good is an excellent score when the underlying knowledge is not acquired? What skills can be developed? What problems can be solved? How is capacity increased? Who wants a doctor who cheated his way through medical school or an accountant who really does not understand financial solutions and controls?

The principle of integrity has existed for thousands of years. When integrity is exercised and actions taken, great progress results. However, the historical record indicates there is a large gap between understanding and implementing integrity as a society or as individuals. It is a matter of building integrity from the inside out, and through this internal integrity-building process both individuals and mankind benefit. Without actively integrating integrity into our lives, we will never build individual capacity beyond the current generation. Mohandas K. Gandhi once said that there are 999 people who believe in honesty for every honest man. Does this same ratio apply to integrity? Thousands of years of experience and words of wisdom have been preserved for our benefit. Must each generation experiment anew with time-proven formulas?

Whenever there is a collapse in capacity, there is a story about failed integrity, such as the executive who received millions of dollars in unauthorized loans from his corporation at his shareholders' expense. What was he thinking? Many executives have deceived themselves, the public, board of directors and shareholders into believing that the correct principles of doing business were being practiced when they were not. When this happens, the house of cards tumbles and capacity crumbles.

On the other side of the equation, one CEO of a public company demonstrated integrity in his every fiber. Jim Donald has been a profound influence on many. I asked him on the day of his retirement, "To what do you owe your incredible success and the success your company has experienced against such great odds?"

His instructive answer was, "I always decide to do the right thing. You will always know what you should do. A voice of conscience will inevitably whisper to you if you are receptive. The difference is determined when you decide to do the right thing—the thing you know you should do as opposed to a course of action that would rationalize away the whisper of conscience. I owe all my success to doing what I know I should do in every decision."[3]

Peter Drucker, a popular management consultant, once said, "Management is doing things right. Leadership is doing the right thing."[4]

Contrast this to the experience of shareholders, employees, and customers of companies that have exhibited a lack of integrity. These are stories of greed, collapse, and despair. Many of these stories are included in this book. In most cases, names have been excluded. It is the story that is important. As you review them, you will notice the relationship between capacity and integrity.

The tales of errant organizations are filled with deception, even self-deception at the highest ranks. One example of this deception is the case of a major public health institution. At least sixteen executives were accused by prosecutors of scheming to inflate profits at the operation of physical therapy, outpatient surgery, and diagnostic imaging centers. Authorities claim that these executives inflated earnings by over $2 billion. After manipulating the financial statements for eleven years, one of the senior officers advised the CEO that they needed to abandon their earnings manipulation. In response, he CEO allegedly arrogantly replied " . . . not until I sell my stock!" The CEO was later ordered by a judge to repay the $25 million in loans he had taken from the company. He was indicted on charges that he directed the fraud designed to boost the company's stock price and to bankroll an extravagant lifestyle that included a Lamborghini, a 92-foot yacht, and paintings by Picasso and Renoir.[5]

If these types of organizations are to recover, they will

---

[3] James Donald, Chairman and CEO of DSC Communications Corporation

[4] Peter F. Drucker (1909-2005) One of America's early and influential thinkers and a writer on the subject of management theory and practice.

[5] Washington Post, Sept. 30, 2004.

have to be rebuilt on principles of integrity. External bandages won't do the job! Integrity must be built from the inside; it must be a part of the character of each individual.

Honesty is clearly the best policy. Even so, honesty is not enough. Sometimes we can be honestly engaged in conduct that is deviant from correct principles. Consider the child who rebels against doing homework because he or she honestly does not like to do homework. This course, though honest, leads to a reduction in personal capacity, wasted time, and wasted effort.

Integrity is much more than basic honesty. It is the incorporation of the correct principles that govern a system into your life or organization. It is the internalization of the principle. It is the internalization of all correct principles into your life, one by one, step by step, that will give you the power to act effectively and efficiently.

***Therefore, our life's adventure
should be an anxious engagement
in discovering truth and living in accordance with truth.***

If we refuse to rationalize, we will discover that truth is the common path for each person on the earth to follow, and there is but one truth. Individual reality is a rationalization of the self-deceived. Though individual circumstances vary, all walk the path of truth even though they are experiencing very different things along the way. Live in accordance with truth, and you will have great capacity. Do not live in accordance with truth, and truth will destroy your capacity.

There is a direct relationship between integrity and

capacity at the system level. A fully integrated system has more capacity than a partially integrated system. Many have spent their professional careers focusing on corporate organizations and business activity.

Success in these fields involves the integration of time, principles, intelligence, skills, leadership, innovation, people, systems, commitments, performances, audits, improvement, contracts, materials, and adherence to rules or laws. It is clear that an organization that integrates all of these elements has more capacity to serve the needs of society than a partially integrated organization. It is also clear that when an organization fails to integrate what it needs, it loses its capacity. Organizations use systems to optimize results.

While it is important to have a personal, family, or corporate mission statement, the critical decision is not merely to have such a statement, but to systematically integrate it into your life, your family, or your corporation. You need to know what actions must be taken to achieve that mission and consistently take those actions without fear or rationalization. It would be good if there were an easier way, but there is not. It takes self-discipline to consistently learn, teach, and follow the rules governing the system for achieving the desired result. Constant reinforcement of values within the system is of key importance. That is why our ministers like to see weekly church attendance. With weekly reinforcement, we are more likely to take consistent action. Someone has described our most serious religious defect as that of being mere Bible Christians, Koran Muslims, etc. That is the case when the primary religious teachings are in the Bible or the Torah or the Koran and not in us.

Political power is developed through the exercise of

integrity. A classic paradox in life is so many people try to grab power without integrity. Tyrants and traitors have long sought political and corporate power without integrity. They use fear mongering. They may use physical power over the acts, but never over the hearts of their people. One needs to look no further than the events that have taken place in Egypt and the Middle East. Their reigns have never lasted or resulted in the advancement or capacity seen in the nations that have adopted and integrated correct principles.

One of the things we sometimes hear in the press is, "Leave this person or that person alone. His personal life (such as affairs outside of his marriage covenant) should have no impact on his corporate or political or sports capabilities." This is mass self-deception. If a man rationalizes in his most sacred promises to his spouse, it certainly reflects his ability to rationalize away his promises to his constituents. Everyone rationalizes to cover their failure to live up to their standards. People with integrity catch themselves and hold themselves accountable.

Why has the United States of America gained such power and capacity? It is because the United States and other free countries were founded upon God-given, inalienable rights, belief in free agency, and the adoption of true and correct principles. They were supported by a foundation of freedom of the press and freedom of religion. Through these freedoms and the adoption of protective patent and copyright laws, the discovery and integration of truth in the physical, emotional, financial, social and spiritual aspects of life are promoted.

***Free countries are founded on a basis of
individual freedom to experiment with and adopt or reject
the principles or truths discovered.***

As long as these basic freedoms are protected, the United States will continue to grow in capacity and power, as will all free nations that actually act in accordance with powerful truths. We will see many nations catch up with the United States by adopting these principles.

Compare the free world to nations that are based on tyranny or governed by dictators. Dictators establish and enforce rules that must be adopted by the governed people. The rules are generally not based on truth, but often on greed. They do not encourage the people to gain power or capacity, because the natural result would be the exercise of that power to overthrow any regime that maintains power by physical threat or violence.

Contrast, for example, the former Soviet Union, where dictators made the rules, with the United States of America, where the people make the rules. In December of 1991, the world saw the once-powerful Soviet Union come to an abrupt end. The totalitarian government led by Lenin, Stalin, Khrushchev and Gorbachev was dismantled, and the many republics that comprised the Soviet Union went their own separate ways. For over 70 years, the Communist Party had controlled the Soviet Union, running all state-owned businesses and quelling any resistance by force. In many ways, the Communist-controlled Soviet Union was a 70-year experiment in economics versus the incentives of free enterprise. The imposed socialistic policies with very little private ownership and incentive stood in stark contrast to the democratic societies of the United States, Japan, and other countries where freedom existed for people to gain capacity. Only since its demise, has the world discovered that the once-thought-to-be-strong Soviet Union had been in economic chaos for many years. Even generating enough food to eat had been a major undertaking in most of the countries that made up the former Soviet Union.

Indeed capitalism, where incentives to work, build, innovate and create prevailed over Communism. Today, realizing that freedom and incentives must exist, the former Soviet Union states are moving their countries to capitalistic, market-driven economies though dictators still lurk in the shadows. China has sky-rocketed economically since their adoption of free market economics. Correct principles do matter!

Many organizations and families are run on a similar type of command and control model that is exhibited in dictatorship governments and in the industrial age, where many managers only desired thoughtless drones. These organizations and families can never develop the same level of capacity of those who teach and systematically integrate correct principles. The more national leaders, corporate managers, and parents teach correct principles and inspire the voluntary integration of these principles into the very being of individuals, the more we will see an increase in production, knowledge, and happiness. Any power or authority that is not founded and based on the complete and voluntary integration of correct principles will eventually fail.

A critical component of integrity is its voluntary nature. Only the volunteer can develop integrity. No one can develop integrity for us. No one can force us to have integrity. It must be an absolute exercise of free choice. Integrity involves sacrifice, denial, and passion. Sacrifice is the trade-off of something of lesser value for something of higher value or something with immediate perceived value for something with long-term perceived value. Denial is the ability to turn away from any activity contrary to the rules governing systems that incorporate higher or long term values. One always experiences these tradeoffs on the path to developing integrity and increased capacity. Passion is the willingness to suffer in order to achieve something of great value, and as far as we know, only humans can consciously do this.

Integrity is the voluntary assumption of the law.

Remember that integrity requires complete compliance with law, defined here as a cause and effect statement of a correct principle. Any thought, intent, or action that violates a correct principle results in loss of integrity. We are faced with multiple voluntary choices daily to either live in compliance with the law or to violate the law. Either way, we reap the consequences.

Voluntary assumption of the law always results in the positive consequences prescribed by the law. There is no space in the universe that exists without a governing set of laws. There is no escape from correct principles. Rationalization does not release us from the law; it only blinds us to the law. No one can force us to violate or comply with correct principles. We must exercise our free agency and choose. Unfortunately, few people develop complete integrity. To paraphrase an earlier quote, there are nine hundred ninety-nine people who believe in integrity for every one person with complete integrity.

What does this mean for our world? We live in an exciting time where there is much opportunity for expanding capacity. Most nations, corporations, families, and individuals have need to improve their integrity. As they do, they will experience quantum leaps in both capacity and security. People who can solve their problems, produce in accordance with their needs, and serve others will have high levels of self-acceptance and self-respect. They will truly be happy, high-capacity people.

During his term as President of Mexico (2000-2006), President Vincente Fox incorporated a program designed to develop integrity within the Mexican government. His arrival in 2000 marked the arrival of democratic rule after seventy years of rule by his predecessors. His *Law of Information Transparency and Accountability Act* was meant to eradicate corruption. Time will tell whether or not the program will be successful. It will depend on how well it is implemented. It is clear that with such a program, voluntarily adopted and engrained in the hearts of the government ministries, Mexico could develop greater capacity as a nation. With its abundant natural resources, increased integrity could transform Mexico into a major world power. President Fox was able to build the first-ever presidential library in Rancho San Christobal, Guanajuato, Mexico, during his term. Many democratic ideas are stored there for perusal by the Mexican leaders. Unfortunately, as of this writing corruption is still rampant in Mexico. Drug wars and men who lack integrity who are following the scheme of short term gain, will result in their own dramatic failure and in a continuing diminishment of their country, unless this situation can be voluntarily reversed. Hope is not high without integrity being voluntarily integrated into the hearts of the people.

China has flourished as they have adopted some correct principles. At a recent world economic conference, Chinese Premier Wen Jiabao stated, "Companies must be honest and integrity is more precious than gold. Corporate culture of multinational corporations will have a big impact on local cultures."[6]

Many third-world countries still have a system of governmental corruption and greed. These nations do not even

---

[6] Sept. 15, 2010. Chinese Premier Wen Jiabao at the Summer Davos in Tianjin, China

have the capacity to feed their children, even though they do not lack food, and they have the support of caring nations around the world. It is greed and the corruption of correct principles that starve their people physically, emotionally, spiritually and intellectually.

There has been much research linking the corruption of countries with their Gross Domestic Product (GDP) and quality of life in those countries. The research shows that countries with high levels of corruption have low GDP and poor quality of life. Transparency International is a German organization that ranks countries by corruption. Transparency uses a series of surveys to assess corruption. (See listings at *www.transparency.com*). Out of 180 countries, the United States ranked 19th from the top. The ten countries lowest on the scale from bottom up are: Somalia, Afghanistan, Myanmar, Sudan, Iraq, Chad, Uzbekistan, Turkmenistan, Iran, and Haiti. These and other low-ranking countries will never reach their potential as long as they continue to have high levels of government and corporate corruption. The very word *corruption* implies a breach of the rules or laws. We can never truly break a law; it still remains intact. Instead, our failure to comply with a law breaks us.

To illustrate why corrupt countries will never get ahead, let's use the example of a company. A number of years ago, a large automobile manufacturing company experienced a $436 million fraud. That fraud reduced the company's net income for the year from what it would have been by $436 million. Since this company made approximately 10 cents on every dollar of revenue (the rest went to pay for raw materials, labor, advertising, etc.), the company would have had to generate ten times as much as the fraud, or $4 billion, 360 million additional dollars of revenue to restore net income to its pre-fraud level.

If you assume that the company sells its average car for $20,000, the company would have to make and sell an additional 218,000 cars to compensate for the fraud. That fraud hurt the company financially and made it more difficult for the company to compete with other automobile companies. The same is true of countries. Since every dollar of fraud and corruption must be compensated by some multiple of GDP, it is very difficult for corrupt countries to even compete with countries that govern with greater integrity.

As integrity is internalized individually, the character of mankind will dramatically improve. Individuals, families, and nations have the ability to develop capacity beyond imagination. Integrity is the vital component to solving the problems of world hunger, war, and despair. Despair, which literally means lack of hope, is caused by a lack of capacity—capacity to solve problems, address issues, and render effective service. Capacity is increased in proportion to the level of integrity exhibited by individuals as leaders, parents, children, teachers, and students. A person who learns and incorporates every correct principle can have unlimited capacity and power.

So let us begin today our adventure in the purposeful development of capacity by increasing our integrity. It will involve the discovery of correct principles. It will be a lifelong adventure. It will take place in our roles as individuals, parents, families, leaders, and governments. The pace is not important, but the direction is essential. If we can make 10% shifts in the right direction, it will have dramatic results. Whatever we know to do, that is what we must consistently and always do. N ever give up in the quest to develop complete integrity. It can be done and will be worth the effort! In the following chapters you will gain a better understanding of integrity and its relationship to capacity, security, and self-respect. Just as the physical body can develop capacity through exercise, you will learn how to strengthen your integrity or your ability to consistently act in accordance with correct principles.

Are you ready?

CHAPTER 2

YOUR PERSONAL CAPACITY IS UNLIMITED

**You can achieve anything
if you know what to do
and you do it.**

In his book, *Outliers, The Story of Success*, (2008), Malcolm Gladwell makes a well-reasoned case for the 10,000 hour rule. This rule states that if you do something for a cumulative 10,000 hours, you will become an expert in that thing. This is true for the development of integrity. Practice integrity in order to get good at it. As I lecture around the country on the subject of leading with integrity, I often ask how many people in the room feel like they have strong integrity. Most hands go up.

We want to feel that we have integrity. Since integrity is always doing the right thing in the right way, a better question to measure integrity would be, "How many think that you always do the right thing in the right way?" Fewer hands would be raised. By the end of our discussion, when that same question is asked, most people feel they can do much more to increase integrity in their lives.

There are multiple weight loss and training exercises one can do at the gym, or even at home, to achieve physical power and general health. These exercises, if actually done consistently for sufficient periods of time, will increase physical capacity. What if there were similar exercises you could perform to increase your emotional, spiritual, intellectual, financial, and social capacity? What if you could become so self-assured, so confident in your abilities to clear away obstacles, so sure of who you are and how you see yourself— that you could turn your focus to the needs of others? What if you could truly learn to respect yourself, to trust yourself, to love yourself?

Just as there are exercises for increasing your physical stamina and strength, there are exercises that will increase your emotional, spiritual, intellectual, financial, and social capacity.

The key to increasing capacity is to increase integrity.
Integrity is the honest incorporation
of correct principles into your life.

The capacity building process described in this book is an exercise in increasing integrity. It has long been the good leader's desire to help individuals, families, organizations and societies be more successful. My route to this objective has been through a study of business management, sociology, social psychology, organizational behavior, and law.

***Laws are the relationships
between actions and outcomes.***

Once you know what to do to achieve a certain outcome (the law), all that stands between you and the desired outcome is the honest incorporation of the action (integrity). As you integrate correct laws and principles, you will have greater capacity and power within the system, and you will accomplish more and more.

How often do we go to an inspiring presentation or seminar, come home fired up to adopt new practices in our lives, and then gradually fall back in to our old habits? While every inspiring presentation can be worth the effort, and many teach powerful, correct principles—actually adopting new-found habits into your life can be difficult. The limitation, it seems, lies within us. The limitation, however, can be overcome, and our capacity to implement new behaviors can grow and improve through regular exercise.

Increasing capacity has been talked about by many great philosophers and leaders throughout time. There are several books about the core principles and habits that result in success. This book is about the relationship between **capacity** and **integrity**. It is about a specific process that you can use to increase your capacity to adopt the principles and habits of success into your own life. It is based on law. Results are always predicated on obedience to law. That is what law is. It is a statement of cause and effect. If you apply the process, your capacity to do everything will increase. If you do this, then consistent results will follow.

The core principles and habits involved in incorporating integrity into your life are not something new. They are time-tested. Each generation does not have to discover them anew. It is by adopting those principles and habits into our own lives that we can become who and what we want to become. Consider the principles at work regarding the context of natural laws.

"For every action, there is an equal and opposite reaction." This is the statement by Isaac Newton of a natural law. Natural laws are sometimes most easily observed in the physical universe, but they are equally applicable in the emotional, spiritual, intellectual, financial and social universes.

A basic natural law is something that can be stated as follows:

For every exercise of independent will, there is a set consequence.

While you are free to choose your actions (or lack of actions), you are not free to choose the consequences of those actions or non-actions. Every time we act there will be a consequence that results. It is in understanding the truth about these consequences that we recognize the unlimited potential that we all have. The personal capacity building process unlocks doors and gives us access to that potential, and it gives us the power to access our unlimited potential. Your personal capacity is unlimited since it is determined by your integrity.

Do you honestly integrate natural laws into your own life? You may think to yourself, 'I implement the natural laws in my life, but don't seem to get the results others are getting.' Don't despair! When you can clearly see the law, you will know how to implement it in order to reap the positive consequences you are seeking. If you are getting different results, there is some part of the law evading your current vision.

Research in moral development tells us that there are two ingredients necessary to develop integrity (or any other trait). Researchers refer to these two elements as: (1) modeling and (2) labeling.

Modeling is being a proper example and labeling is teaching and training. In the business world, modeling is often referred to as the tone at the top and labeling is accomplished with codes of conduct and other ethical statements, training, and practices. The research conclusions indicate that when these two ingredients are not consistently positive, negative activities occur. For example, an organization that has poor tone at the top and/or poor labeling will usually have more fraud and other ethical problems than an organization that has a positive tone at the top and a strong code of conduct.

The same is true in our lives. You can work hard to teach your children to be honest, but when you install and use a radar detector in your automobile to avoid getting a speeding ticket or you receive too much change at the grocery store and fail to give it back to the cashier, your bad model may destroy all the teaching you have done. If you are guilty of inconsistent modeling and labeling in cases like these, it shouldn't surprise you when your son or daughter cheats on a test in school, shoplifts from a store, is disrespectful of authority, or wrecks your car going 90 miles per hour.

Master teachers recognize the need to use both modeling and labeling in their teaching. In fact, most of the world's great leaders not only taught what was right, but they were excellent models. Consider Jesus Christ who taught with parables (labeling) and by forgiving trespassers, healing sinners, cleansing the temple, etc. (modeling).

A story is told of Mahatma Gandhi:

"A mother once brought her child to him, asking him to tell the young boy not to eat sugar, because it was not good for his diet or his developing teeth. Gandhi replied, "I cannot tell him that. But you may bring him back in a month." The mother was angry as Gandhi moved on, brushing her aside. She had traveled some distance, and had expected the mighty leader to support her parenting. She had little recourse, so she left for her home. One month later she returned, not knowing what to expect. The great Gandhi took the small child's hands into his own, knelt before him, and tenderly communicated, "Do not eat sugar, my child. It is not good for you." Then he embraced him and returned the boy to his mother. The mother, grateful but perplexed, queried, "Why didn't you say that a month ago?" "Well," said Gandhi, "a month ago, I was still eating sugar."[7]

If you desire to develop integrity in yourself, your employees, or your children, you must teach the law and model how living the law gets the desired consequence. To not do so

---

[7] http://www.wdsi.ca/articles/trust-integrity.html

is to settle for a life that lacks integrity and teaches others to do the same.

We are all subject to the truths of natural laws. The consequences of our actions are unavoidable. Since natural laws in the physical universe are easier to observe, let's start there. At an inspiring seminar on nutrition and exercise, a series of vital natural laws that govern the body were presented. With the understanding that weight is a function of the metabolism of calories taken in versus calories expended, as impacted by the fat storage hormone known as insulin, you learned that by increasing the expenditure of calories through exercise and reducing the total caloric consumption, particularly the calories from carbohydrates that trigger insulin, you will lose weight. The seminar leader may have been very effective in personalizing how these laws apply to your situation, and the words resonated within you as truth. As a result of the seminar presentations and your involvement, you gained an incredible amount of knowledge about the subject, and were enthusiastic and determined to apply the principles learned immediately. For the first few weeks after attending, you were keenly conscious of decisions made about food and exercise based on the natural laws learned at the seminar, but old habits crept back into your daily rituals. When you first violated those principles, and felt guilty because you knew better, your mind immediately went to work on inventing rationales which would make you feel better about your choice to violate the laws of weight loss .

> "I don't think it was working like it should."

> "I am so stressed. I need my comfort food."

"Certainly I can't make my friends feel uncomfortable by refusing the delicious chocolate cake they made."

"It works for other people, but my body type is different and it just doesn't work for me."

These thoughts made it easier to not follow the laws learned, while the seminar became a distant memory and you reverted to your old habits. You may rationalize that you like who and what you are, and that there was no need to change or adapt to these natural laws in your life, or you convinced yourself that it just didn't work for you. Therefore, you continue to achieve the same results and consequences, because you revert back to the same behaviors. Integrity is a habit, but as illustrated here, so is a lack of integrity.

In the quest for personal development, many have experienced this very scenario several times. They have rationalized away their capacity. It is only through increased integrity that they can avoid this result.

***The good news is that
you can increase your integrity!***

This book will teach you how to incorporate timeless natural laws and principles into your life and how to understand and plan the path that leads to success, how to clear the obstacles and rationalizations from the path, how to walk the path, and how to enjoy the results. It will explain how to achieve results in each area of your life.

Would you like to expand your financial capacity?

Expand your emotional capacity? Expand your physical capacity? Expand your spiritual capacity? Use this process in all areas of your life including your career, personal, family, and community.

It is possible to break the cycle that enforces negativity in your life, learn how to overcome rationalization, and make and keep commitments through a regular, defined program. In the following pages you will find that integrity is a prerequisite for unleashing capacity.   As you increase your integrity, self-trust, self-respect, and a positive self-image follow. You will explore ways to develop the tools you can use to increase your integrity. Building integrity is a process accomplished in small steps.

As you work to develop integrity, don't be delusional about your progress. Remember an important truth that behavioral scientists teach:

***We often tend to judge ourselves by our intentions
and other people by their actions.***

None of us are as good as our intentions. Most of us intend to get up earlier, eat better, exercise more, and have more patience and so forth. We just don't get it done. If we could be objective and judge ourselves by our actions, we would realize that we often give ourselves far too much credit. Similarly, we often don't value others enough, because we give them no credit for their intentions.

***The truth is that none of us is as good
as we think we are,
nor are we as bad
as other people think we are.***

Take parenting as an example. You might think you are a really good parent. Yet, if you are like most people, you have probably suffered periods where you were a workaholic or for some other reason didn't spend enough time with your children. During those periods, you still considered yourself to be a good parent because your intentions were good. Unfortunately, good intentions don't do nearly as much for your children as those good intentions make you feel good about yourself.

Success, to a large degree, in business, families, and societies in the 21st century depends on productivity. Yet many people, who are honest with themselves, know that they could be much more productive. They hear an inner voice whisper that they could do and be much more than they are. Others, fearful of failure, have closed off any feeling for becoming more productive. The shutters in their minds close off, and they can no longer visualize their true self. Many people have shut religion, education, advancement, and even social interaction out of their lives by saying, "I'm just too busy with my job or personal life to do any more." Perhaps they declare, "I just don't see myself doing that!"

Yet we all know people who have great capacity to produce in their job well, perform their church responsibilities well, and nurture and protect their family environment well. In addition, these same people are the ones who volunteer in their social environments, develop their talents, and take on extraordinary projects at the same time.

***The interesting thing is that
we all have the same amount of time.***

There are 24 hours in the day and every hour has 60 minutes. No one can have less or more. Time is fixed. How can time possibly limit one more than another?

The fact is that we are not limited by time. You might say then, that we are limited by the events that we stack up in a set time. Logically, we can only do so much. This is true. But who is really accomplishing more during the allotted time? You or the person you most admire for his or her capacity? If you are honest with yourself, you know that each of us has potential for greater capacity, but, we are not always honest with ourselves. Our minds work in marvelous, complex ways! What our minds allow us to conceive and know about ourselves is sometimes limited. This reluctance to be honest with ourselves is one of the chief causes for capacity limitations. It is a lack of integrity.

In the following chapters we will explore our basic needs, our capacity to realize those needs in our lives, and the limitations that we place on ourselves that keep us from attaining those needs. The wonderful thing is that we are blessed with free agency—the ability to take independent action, to challenge our own thinking, to level with ourselves or to reconcile our limitations. Through the application of the principles and the exercises set forth in this book, you can increase your capacity to act, to take advantage of your potential, and to meet your basic needs. Best of all, you will know yourself better and you will like what you become.

Integrity Exercises

Here are 10 exercises you can do to increase your integrity:

(1) Push Up

Set a small goal that is easy to achieve, like doing 10 physical push-ups a week, and consistently do it for one year without missing.

(2) Squat

Set a goal to meditate or pray for at least 10 minutes 3 times a week and do it consistently for one year.

(3) Pull Up

Set a goal to go without eating for two meals one day a month and consistently do it for one year.

(4) Step-up

Set a goal to make your bed each morning and do it consistently for one year.

(5) Plank.

Set a goal to sit down and actually talk with someone special to you for at least 30 minutes once a week . . . not texting, not a phone call, but face to face. Do this for one year.

(6) One Leg Dead Lift

Set a goal to update your knowledge base in your vocational area by reading journals or non-fiction books (at least two per month for one year).

(7)   Stick Up

Take your significant other on a regular date night once a week, even if it's simply an evening walk n' talk. Plan to continue your ongoing courtship on these dates—do not use the time to discuss kids or family problems. Never miss for a year!

(8) T Push Up

Put 10% of each paycheck into a special savings account. At the end of the year, set aside a portion of your savings and enjoy a special event or trip.

(9) V Up and Roll

Get a planner and schedule your actions into a calendar for one year. Constantly evaluate so that if daily plans change, you are still addressing your key goals.

(10) Shoulder Press Push Up

 Set a goal to uplift another person each and every day. It can be as simple as a phone call, a compliment, or a service rendered. Do it for one year.

CHAPTER 3

WHAT IS
INTEGRITY?

**Integrity is the honest and complete
incorporation of principles
that are correct
into your life.**

Integrity is the quality of always doing what you know you should do. Think about it. How many of the things that you know you should do, do you always do and never skip? Think for a minute how you would feel about yourself if you consistently did what you know you should do.

How do you know if you can trust another person? Generally, it is based on your experience with the consistency of that person's conduct in the past. There was a time when no one felt the need for a written contract. A person's word was all that was required. Enemies would settle conflicts by accepting mere verbal representations from people who, hours before, were fighting to the death. Commercial transactions would take place based on a verbal representation and a handshake. A recommended book to illustrate the value of trust and its impact on capacity is *The Speed of Trust* by Stephen M. R. Covey.

Even today, there are some people and businesses that have so much integrity, that they can be trusted with anything. Bill Child, former owner of the RC Willey furniture stores in Utah, Idaho, and Nevada is an example. RC Willey is the largest home furnishings retailer west of the Mississippi. In today's tough competitive world, RC Willey and Bill Child stand tall as leaders of a firm with strong ethical values.

Rufus Call Willey started the business in 1932 by selling appliances out of his pickup truck door-to-door. In 1949, R.C. opened his first store in Syracuse, Utah (at the time, a very small town of less than 300 people). R.C. established a strategy of offering better quality at the absolute lowest prices.

In June 1954, shortly after graduating from college, William (Bill) Child took over the reins of the business from his father-in-law, R.C. This decision came after R.C. was diagnosed with pancreatic cancer; R.C. died in September of that same year.

In 1995, RC Willey was acquired for $175 million by Warren Buffett, and fell under the umbrella of Buffett's holding company, Berkshire Hathaway. Although Buffett is one of the primary owners of RC Willey, he still keeps Bill Child to manage the company as he sees fit. Warren Buffett has publicly stated that every transaction with Bill Child has been made on a handshake.

Ever since the company was founded, RC Willey has established a strong reputation for being an ethical company. As an example of its ethical decisions, when a warranty company declared bankruptcy shortly after RC Willey had paid $192,000 for warranty service, RC Willey could have easily told customers that the bankrupt insurance company was responsible for the warranty. RC Willey didn't do that. Instead Bill Child decided to back all of the warranties, even though RC Willey had no legal responsibility to do so.

Bill Child afterward said, "It cost us more than $1.5 million over the next five years, but we just felt it was the morally right thing to do."

Another moral and ethical stance taken by RC Willey was its *Closed on Sunday* policy. Rufus Call Willey and Bill Child were both religious men, who never did business on Sundays, in accordance with their Sabbath beliefs. However, when RC Willey decided to expand to Idaho, Warren Buffett did not want to maintain their *Closed on Sunday* policy. Buffett understood a true fact that Sunday is often the biggest retail day of the week when many consumers are most likely to shop.

Bill Child believed Sabbath observance to be such a correct principle that he offered to invest $11 million of his own money to build the Idaho store, and promised to sell it back to Berkshire at cost without interest if the venture succeeded. If it failed, Bill would keep the store and personally absorb any losses.[8]

The expansion into Idaho was an immediate success. Shortly after the Boise opening, Bill Child brazenly suggested expansion into Las Vegas, while still maintaining the *Closed on Sunday* policy. Warren Buffett was even more nervous about such a move. Yet, after the success of the Boise store, Buffett let Child expand into Henderson (a neighboring town to Las Vegas). Again, the result was positive.

In Warren Buffett's annual letter to shareholders in 2001, he stated that the Henderson store "outsells all others in the R.C. Willey chain, doing a volume of business that far

---

[8] http://www.berkshirehathaway.com/letters/2001pdf.pdf

exceeds the volume of any competitor and that is twice what I had anticipated."[9] Jokingly, at the end of this remark Buffett stated, "Today, when I pontificate about retailing, Berkshire people just say, 'What does Bill think?'"[10]

Great rewards and dividends result from following correct principles. In today's society, we not only have to rely on written contracts, but they must address every aspect of a proposed transaction with painstaking detail. Even so, few contracts are lived up to. Think of the waste caused in our society by this lack of integrity! We spend billions of dollars each year trying to get people to do what they promised to do in the first place. We waste much time and effort when people do not do what they say they will do: the low-capacity way to do things. The good news is that gains can be made if we, as individuals, increase our integrity. We are interdependent. When someone does not do what they know they should do, time and resources are wasted, and all of society suffers; when the opposite occurs, all of society benefits.

Take the simple example of being on time. When a meeting is supposed to start at 2:00 P.M., we depend on one another to be there at the appointed time. If someone is not there, it wastes the time and resources of others who were there and ready to begin. You might think this does not really matter much, but it does, especially when it is being repeated hundreds of thousands of times each day throughout the organization or across the country! Meetings are a huge investment of time, and the #1 time commitment of most organizations. The top cause of inefficient meetings is not starting on time. When people make good use of their time in meetings, there is a terrific return on time invested. When meetings are inefficient, objectives are not

---

[9] http://www.berkshirehathaway.com/letters/2001pdf.pdf

[10] http://www.berkshirehathaway.com/letters/2001pdf.pdf

met. Starting late and having to wait for participants is a prescription for non-productivity, inaction, and a lack of return on time invested. Capacity is diminished even by this small failure to be punctual. The GNC (Gross National Capacity) is diminished, group capacity is diminished, and individual capacity is diminished. Everyone is affected.

One successful leader has a practice of starting every meeting fifteen minutes early—not just on time! By doing so, he has found everyone is on time, meetings don't last too long and much more is accomplished. In this organization, even being on time means that you have missed important discussions and decisions.

Surely everyone knows that they should do what they promise they will do, whether or not they are compensated for their promises. It is the basic form of integrity. It is the basic culmination of promise and action. To go a step further, to really incorporate integrity into our lives, we also need to do the things that we know we should do, whether or not a promise has been made.

Contemplate the following story as related by a prominent radio host:

> "As our family was driving through Arizona, we stopped at a service station for fuel. While the car was being serviced, one of the children asked, "Could we have some soda pop?"
>
> I went to the vending machine, inserting one dollar and I got out one bottle. I put in another dollar and I got out another bottle. I put in a third dollar and out came the third bottle,

but somehow a malfunction occurred, and the mechanism didn't lock. Out rolled another bottle; magically, the fourth bottle was free!

As I was returning to the car to hand out the treats, I thought to myself, 'They charge too much for this stuff anyway.'

However, I have a little mental night-watchman on duty up there in my brain someplace who started to make a fuss, and hc said, 'Look, if you're going to be a crook, you had better get more than just one dollar out of it.'"

**Integrity is not merely "being true to what you believe"
Rather it is "believing and doing what is true."**

In order to realize integrity in families or organizations, integrity must be developed from the inside-out. There is no outside-in method that will instill integrity. In 2002, as a result of several highly-publicized frauds (Enron and WorldCom), Congress imposed stiff new regulations on the senior management of public corporations. These regulations, known as the Sarbanes Oxley Act (often referred to as SOX), determine which records require storage and for how long and are meant to protect shareholders and the general public from accounting errors and fraudulent practices. Sarbanes Oxley and other regulations may help establish the rules, but they are merely a bandage for the wounds. The wounds must heal from the inside.

Until individual workers understand that following the rules is a requirement for their own increased power and capacity, perceived pressures and opportunities will prevail upon them to take shortcuts. Organizations should consider devoting significant resources to educate their employees about integrity and its relationship to capacity. Teaching true doctrine is the fastest and most efficient way to influence behavior. Individuals must make the connection voluntarily on their own. Integrity cannot be forced; it must be self-absorbed and the only way to do it is to invest resources in education. Ideally, the importance of this organizational training will spill over into the homes and lives of the employees.

Children today are not always receiving this vital training in their homes. Some children are–but many are not. Mothers and fathers, do you understand the importance of teaching the why should we do's in your homes? There is no better way to build self-respect and love in your children than in teaching them what they should do–inspiring and motivating those children to voluntarily do what they know they should. If young people develop a habit of doing what they know they should do, they will enjoy self-respect and self-confidence as they accomplish their goals.

There is not a single person on the earth who possesses complete integrity. Everybody has integrity to varying degrees, just as we all have unique qualities and differences that make life interesting. Some people have a high intelligence quotient. Others have a wonderful ability to control their emotions and impulses. Each of us varies in our talents and abilities. One thing we all have in common, however, is the ability to increase our integrity. If we are striving to do everything we know we should do, both our integrity and our capacity, or power, will increase. Perfection is a process of striving and making incremental shifts. A friend's mother used to tell him, "Never rest until your good is better, and your better is best."

When we speak of physical materials we equate integrity with strength. This concept is self evident in the aerospace business. Integrity is a critically important component in the manufacture of aircraft. Weakness anywhere in the structure cannot be tolerated. There is no margin for error. The entire structure must be sound. There can be no weakness in the outer skin of the aircraft, nor weakness in the bolts, framework, or engine. In order to have the power or capacity the aircraft needs to do the job for which it is designed, it requires complete integrity. Are we not like the aircraft? Can we really do the job for which we were designed if we lack integrity in any part of our structure? Will we have the full capacity for leadership, the strength to endure, or the power to motivate and manage without complete integrity? The answer is clearly "No!" A chain is only as strong as its weakest link. Is it reasonable that if we lack integrity in the emotional area our power in the financial area will be limited? Is it reasonable that if we lack integrity in the spiritual area of our life, our social power will be limited? Can these things limit our capacity in our careers?   The answer is "Yes!"

Integrity implies wholeness, a complete structural strength. We cannot neglect any area of our existence. The rationale for this statement is important to understand.

In order to have integrity, by definition, one must be able to understand and see correct principles.

Many people are blind to correct principles. This is illustrated by an example. Jim was entering his teenage years. He lived in a home with a mother and a father who loved him. His mother had always been diligent in keeping an orderly home. The parents had explained to all of their children the principles upon which an orderly home operates. Their expectation was that each member of the family would contribute by taking some of the workload. One of the rules was that everyone was to make his own bed prior to leaving for the day. Jim, of course, knew the rule. Every day as he got dressed, the thought crossed his mind that he should make his bed. Most days, however, he did not do so. What do you think his thoughts were?

'I am so busy with my activities during the day, I shouldn't be expected to make the bed.'

'I would make the bed, but I do not have the time.'

'I am really applying myself to my studies and doing a good job and that should be enough.'

'I really am a good kid.'

These are all rationalizations of the truth, but now Jim is beginning to believe them. The truth is that the bed should be made in order for the home to properly function at full capacity. When he doesn't do his part, someone else has to take on his responsibility. However, it gets worse. Not only will Jim rationalize about how good he is, but he will rationalize how bad others are. Such thoughts as the following may go through his mind:

'My mother is so lazy. She is home all day with nothing to do and can't even expend the effort to make my bed for me. Why doesn't she just come up and make my bed?'

'She is a bad mother. She is inconsiderate.'

'Mom doesn't understand how lucky she is that I am a good son in so many other ways.'

'She and Dad just make up these rules to get us to work. They think we kids are slaves.'

'It's their house; they should keep it clean and neat.'

'I am beginning not to like them very much. I'll show them.'

All of these negative rationalizations are false, but Jim now believes them. He must think of himself as the good guy and someone else as the bad guy in order to live with his decision not to make his bed. He is now blind to the truth, and he is deceiving himself. He will now begin to act on his self-deceiving beliefs, rather than on correct principles. This illustration reinforces how serious the judging phenomenon is that we described earlier.

As we stated, we all judge ourselves by our intentions and others by their actions. Surely, Jim intended to make his bed. He just didn't get it done. The way we judge ourselves and others leads to the destructive thoughts and actions described.

**We can increase our capacity
by shrinking the difference between
our intentions and our actions
and by rationalizing less
when we don't accomplish our intentions.**

This story illustrates how easily a small event in one's life can have a profound impact. This is especially true if the same thing happens day after day. Unfortunately this is a story that is repeated many times every day throughout the world. Can we even imagine the cumulative decrease in capacity brought about by the lack of integrity of a rebellious child?

But who is to blame? Blame is the calling card of rationalization and self-deception. That is not the important question to ask. The fact is parents are not equipped with an instruction book, and children have to discover the value of integrity. The fastest way to influence correct behavior is to teach correct principles. Jim's parents should teach the principle and the purpose of each member of the family making their own beds, and why it contributes so much to the capacity of both the individual and the home. Merely having a rule that Jim and the other children make their beds isn't sufficient.   Understanding how making their beds increases the capacity of the home and everyone in it leads to increased health, harmony, respect, organization and discipline.

Leading with integrity is one of the most important duties of a parent. The home is the ideal environment to teach the simple lessons of integrity. No great harm is done from an unmade bed, but it is an opportunity to teach integrity and to give it a daily exercise. A child who has learned the lessons of integrity in the home is well-equipped to run the businesses, churches, nations, and institutions of tomorrow.

Robert Fulghum wrote a book entitled *All I Really Need To Know I Learned In Kindergarten*. The lessons he conveys in that book go a long way toward helping us understand integrity. In the sand pile at kindergarten, Fulghum learned life's important lessons including the importance of sharing, playing fair, not hitting people, putting things back where you found them, cleaning up your own mess, not taking things that aren't yours, and saying "sorry" when you hurt somebody. These are true principles that will greatly increase our capacity once they are integrated into our hearts, minds, and souls and then consistently put into action. In routinely doing these things, they become habits.

Whether in a family or a corporation, teaching integrity is critical to developing integrity. After all the teaching, instruction, and learning has taken place, integrity is still a choice. It is the ultimate choice. As we exercise our integrity muscles by choosing to comply with correct principles, we will better understand the principles, or laws, and why they work to produce a more efficient and effective society. It will then become easier to choose to comply with other correct principles instead of rationalizing. Integrity is a habit.

Integrity adds to the predictability of any form of society and predictability is important! There can never be security without predictability. No one would drive down the highway if predictability were not important. Without it, you could never trust the oncoming car to stay in its lane or to stop at a red light. Integrity is the voluntary incorporation of correct principles and the systems that they govern into our very being. It is the core principle of life.

It has been said that obedience is the first law under heaven, but the deeper meaning of this saying sometimes escapes us. It is the recognition and application of truth (or obedience to the laws) that gives capacity and power to people both as individuals and as groups. The utilization of integrity in the everyday choices that all men and women make enables them to truthfully recognize law, without any rationalization, and to strictly follow the law in order to enjoy its consequences. Those consequences will be greater knowledge, power, and happiness with a valuable side benefit: the discovery of more laws with their attendant benefits of even greater knowledge, power, and happiness. It is not only that more laws will be discovered, but the process of adapting to those newly-discovered laws will become easier, based on our experience of following each law, step by step, and layer upon layer.

CHAPTER 4

THE RELATIONSHIP BETWEEN INTEGRITY AND SECURITY

If 90% of your doors are locked, you are not secure.

There is a clear relationship between integrity and security; the greater your integrity, the more security you obtain. Security is defined as freedom from danger, fear, and anxiety. Anxiety is aptly defined as painful or apprehensive uneasiness of mind regarding an impending or anticipated bad situation, and self-doubt regarding one's capacity to deal with the problem. Dealing with a situation with confidence makes you feel secure.

Remember, integrity is based on law and there are laws that govern everything in life. There are man-made laws and there are natural laws. Not all of these laws are yet discovered or understood completely; nevertheless, they do exist. Rest assured, there is no space where there is no law. A law is a statement of cause and effect. If you perform y, the result will be x. Statements of cause and effect govern each of the realms of life: financial, physical, emotional, spiritual, social, and intellectual. Not all statements of cause and effect are accurate. A law is a statement of cause and proven effect based on observation over time. Many of these causes and effects have been observed by thousands of people over thousands of years. They are time-tested. In those instances, we can be quite sure that if we do y, then x will be the result. Other statements of cause and effect are not as well-documented or tested. Science refers to these as theses or hypotheses. They relate to causes and effects that are theorized and have not yet been sufficiently observed and tested to be referred to as laws. A thesis or hypothesis is stated as a law for testing purposes.

Dr. Phil McGraw, an American television personality, author, and a former psychologist, has galvanized millions of Americans to get real about their own behavior and create more positive lives. He often challenges people's rationalized hypotheses with the question, "How's that working for you?"

We can discover whether or not cause and effect statements are accurate by observing the results. Mankind has barely scratched the surface of the cause and effect relationships that are available for us to discover. The scientific study of chaos has shown that there are patterns in things we previously thought to be random activities. For example, when analyzed with the power of a computer and plotted, water dripping from a pipe produces an organized pattern, which we can observe, but cannot yet explain.

In 1992, author Margaret Wheatley authored a book entitled *Leadership and the New Science*. This book takes into account discoveries in quantum physics, chaos theory, and biology that challenge our standard way of organizational thinking.

Wheatley states, "Western cultural views of how best to organize and lead (now the methods most used in the world) are contrary to what life teaches. Leaders use control and imposition rather than participative, self-organizing processes. They react to uncertainty and chaos by tightening already feeble controls, rather than engaging people's best capacities to learn and adapt. In doing so, they only create more chaos. Leaders incite primitive emotions of fear, scarcity, and self-interest to get people to do their work, rather than the mere noble human traits of cooperation, caring, and generosity. This has led to this difficult time, when nothing seems to work as we want it to, when too many of us feel frustrated, disengaged, and anxious."[11]

"There is a simpler, finer way to organize human endeavor. I have declared this for many years and have seen it to be true in many places. This simpler way is demonstrated to us in daily life, not the life we see on the news with its unending stories of human grief and sorrow, but what we feel when we experience a sense of life's deep harmony, beauty, and power, of how we feel when we see people helping each other, when we feel creative, when we know we're making a difference, when life feels purposeful."[12]

There is much that has been discovered that applies to cause and effect in the realms of life referenced above. There is enough for us to integrate those discoveries into our lives and gain the capacity we need in order to experience security or freedom from anxiety. Many of these laws are not hard to understand. Most of the important statements of cause and effect were given to us as children by our mothers and fathers. The family institution is one of the most successful and productive institutions of society. Those things that we need to know to be productive adults came to us in the family setting.

---

[11] Interview with Margaret Wheatley by Scott London

[12] Interview with Margaret Wheatley by Scott London

"Be nice to your brother, pick up your things, make your bed, wash your face, take a bath, brush your teeth, share you toys, be respectful to your mother, don't stay out too late, use the buddy system, do your chores, be on time, don't watch too much TV, study hard and get a good education."

These are examples of the things most of us learned as children and young adults. When we obeyed, we were rewarded with positive consequences of safety and security. When we disobeyed, we learned there were negative consequences. The family system is the school-master for us to learn how to successfully integrate systems and the laws that govern them into our lives. It is of great importance that the home is a place of safety and security.

One way of understanding the relationship between integrity and security is in the context of financial management. People who do not understand and integrate the laws that pertain to this realm of life into their behavior are often insecure, have anxiety for the future, and worry they will not have the resources to provide. They live in constant fear, and for security, often hang onto the habits and practices to which they are accustomed. The problem is if that their actions thus far (the cause) have not served their financial interests, the same behavior in the future is unlikely to produce a different result (effect). They are trapped. They lack hope for improvement and do not believe their lot in life can change. Following sound financial laws gives you freedom and security. Ignoring financial laws usually results in large amounts of debt, lack of freedom, and the inability to take control of your life. Nothing is quite as discouraging and debilitating as debt and obligations that one cannot meet. Self-reliance cannot be achieved when you have serious debt. One issue is that through rationalizations these people truly believe that if someone is rich, they must have cheated other people. They no longer believe that they, too, can follow sound financial principles and become financially secure. My wealthy grandfather used to always say, "A million dollars is saved for it to be yours. You can earn it, but until it is saved, it belongs to whoever can get it."[13]

Saving is a sound financial principal that people tend to neglect. Proverbs 22:7 it reads, "The rich ruleth over the poor, and the borrower is servant to the lender."

A wise man once said, "If there is any one thing that will bring peace and contentment into the human heart and into the family, it is to live within our means. If there is any one thing that is grinding and discouraging and disheartening, it is to have debts and obligations that one cannot meet."[14]

We lose options and predictability when we are in debt. We lose security when we do not follow the laws of financial success. This is why the educated always appear to have a potential advantage in life. At least they are exposed to the statements of cause and effect that govern financial dealings. The real question is . . . How many of the laws regarding finance are they willing to adopt into their lives? That is what will determine their security. How consistently are they willing to follow the laws that pertain to financial success? Will they integrate the system and the laws which govern that system into their lives? Educated people realize that once in debt, for example, interest will be their constant companion, every minute of the day. It doesn't rest. It doesn't sleep. And, if you fail to meet its demands, it crushes you. It isn't that interest is always bad. High interest rates are good for net savers and only bad for

---

[13] George Brunt (1876-1956) Grandfather to the author and Idaho pioneer and businessman

[14] Gordon B. Hinckley (1910-2008) Prominent Utah leader and recipient of the Presidential Medal of Freedom

net borrowers. When it comes to money management, interest is like a saw. When used appropriately, it can build a beautiful house or a successful business. When used inappropriately, it can cut your financial stability into pieces and undermine your security.

The element of constancy also factors into the equation of security. Increased integrity times constancy equals an increase in capacity which equals an increase in security. This formula can be written as follows:

Increased Integrity x Constancy = Increased Capacity which produces Increased Security

If you lack constancy, the equation breaks down. Some people are honest 90% of the time, and some people are moral 90% of the time. How secure do you feel at night if 90% of your doors are locked? How secure do you feel if you think you have the capacity to deal with 90% of the critical needs of your children? The only way you can experience real security is by always acting on the things you know that you should do. You must be filled with integrity to enjoy maximum security. Even little breaches cause large issues. A situation where 10% of the doors are unlocked or where you are almost safe is not secure.

As an example of how a lack of integrity leads to a lack of security, consider the case of cheating on income taxes. While the probability of a tax audit by the IRS may be low, cheaters live in constant fear that their returns may be selected for scrutiny.

That was certainly the case, for example, with the pre-1987 tax cheaters who were claiming their pets as dependents. When the government changed the law so that all dependents claimed needed to have social security numbers, these cheaters' returns were exposed and those claiming the dependents were fined and punished.

Think about our equation and its relationship to marital security. It is late at night. You and your spouse have both fallen asleep on the couch in front of the TV. Your spouse has had a busy day and has been feeling a little under the weather. As you both wake up to head off to bed, and you are about to turn off the kitchen light, you notice that the dishes are not done from dinner. You hear a prompting that says, 'I should really do the dishes so my spouse won't have to deal with them before going to bed or in the morning.' What do you do? If you ignore the "should do" prompting, you will find yourself coming up with some rationalization for doing so. In your rationalization you must come up with two sets of logic. One will be directed at your spouse and why he or she is inconsiderate, lazy, a procrastinator etc. They may sound something like this:

> 'She could have easily done the dishes right after dinner, but no, she left them on the table.'

> 'Why! She probably is pretending she didn't see the dishes. She's a phony, a faker!'

The other set of logic will deal with why you are so good. Following are several examples:

> 'I am such a good provider!'

'Why, we wouldn't have even have food to eat
if it hadn't been for the hours of labor I put in.'

'I deserve respect and she should be waiting on
me instead of me helping her when I come home.
I deserve the rest. After all, she's home all day.'

It is from little situations like this when reality gets distorted that great chasms develop. We become blind to the truth when we rationalize in this manner. That blindness causes us to believe something false about our spouses and ourselves. It prevents us from seeing the areas where we need to improve. It halts our forward progress. If you cannot see a need to progress, you won't progress. It is a series of these breaches in integrity that are responsible for most of the divorces that occur in the world. They blind us to reality. They create a fictional reality that we believe is reality. How secure is that?

You may believe all the doors to the house are locked, but if some of them are really not locked, intruders can enter. Often people who believe they are most secure have the least actual security due to their mistaken beliefs. That explains why some people seem to have such self-confidence, but really have nothing to back it up. They believe their own fictions. It is a self-defeating cycle, because they cannot improve where they see no need for improvement.

Marriages work best when there is more selflessness and less selfishness and rationalization. While we may think the spouse is the one who benefits most from unselfish acts, it is really the doer of unselfish acts who is the beneficiary through feelings of accomplishment, satisfaction from being kind, and from the happiness that comes from knowing you did what your heart was telling you to do. There is something magical about service—it always benefits the one giving the service more than the one receiving the service. People who serve, and especially serve those they love, are happy people. People who are selfish and only think of themselves tend to be miserable and unhappy. Selfishness is a self-defeating cycle, because one cannot improve his state when he is unwilling to take action in accordance with the laws that govern happiness. Selfish people sink deeper and deeper into their own rationalizations.

This situation is similar to the rationalization cycle we discussed earlier. Most of us believe we are better than we are, because we judge ourselves by our intentions. Our intentions are always better than our actions, and so we rationalize the difference. For example, a friend who traveled frequently once told me, "I think I'm a pretty good father." However, when he was forced to calculate how much time he was spending with his children and to judge himself by his actions, he realized that it was only his intentions and his ability to rationalize that allowed him to think of himself as a good father. This exercise caused him to reschedule his time to spend more time with his children.

Security is a result of integrity. When we apply our focus to real situations, and to the actual facts—then we can be effectively secure. Lawyers are trained first to understand the facts. This is no haphazard process. No case can be made that is not based on the facts. No situation can be understood if the true facts are not understood. The process that lawyers follow to analyze a case can be instructive. First, the facts must be clear. The worst thing clients can do for their cases is to misrepresent the facts to their attorneys. Next, the attorney must analyze what issues are raised by the facts. The issues must be looked at in light of the rules or laws that govern the issues. The law must be applied to the issues, and conclusions made accordingly.

Decisions based on facts and data are always better than

those made on emotion. Consider two simple examples. Let's say you want to reward your top employee for his or her effort in the company. If you can define what it means to be successful and what outcome measures you will use to assess productivity according to that definition, you can make an objective decision about who should receive the award. Not only will your decision be supported by even those who didn't get the award, but the process will have integrity and the award will be meaningful. If you have defined the outcome measures accurately so that they motivate employees to do what is important to the success of the company, and if the award is meaningful and significant, giving the award will have a very positive effect on employee productivity. Conversely, if you give the award to an employee without data to support your decision, other employees will attribute all kinds of excuses for them not getting the award such as 'He likes the recipient better than me or he is playing favorites again.' Data-based decisions are always the most meaningful and defensible. They also result in the most security for an employee who then knows his award was earned and the employer who has justly encouraged real contribution.

As another example . . . for years retail stores believed that their most serious fraud problem was shoplifting. They spent hundreds of millions of dollars installing cameras, having secret shoppers who were really watching for shoplifting, and implementing other preventive and detective measures. However, after retail theft had been studied thoroughly, it became obvious that only approximately 30% of inventory losses in retail firms were caused by customer shoplifting while employee theft accounted for 70% of the losses. This realization, based on data–that it was the back door rather than the front door that was the problem–led to better fraud prevention expenditures and reduced losses. In this case, making data-based decisions led to security and lower losses. To have real security we must follow a similar process in our lives. The most serious problem is that sometimes we are blind to the facts. "There is nothing so insane or futile than to resist what is."[15]

Because of our choices, we often begin to rationalize the real facts to the point that we can no longer see them. This is true of the alcoholic. He starts to see himself as physically all right or only as a social drinker. Soon he actually believes his rationalizations are the facts. The alcoholic is left acting out a destructive pattern of behavior that jeopardizes his relationships, his job, his health, his fortune, and his family. If we miss the facts, we miss the real issues. If we miss the real issues, we cannot apply the law or reach a true conclusion.

Have you ever had a conversation with someone who you felt was entirely missing the issue? They probably were. A person who cannot see the true facts does not have the capacity to act on the true facts. Why? They cannot see them. They do not have the capacity to deal with the real issues. Why? They cannot see the real issues. These people are likely to apply the wrong laws. In fact they usually make up their own set of laws. These faulty laws sound like:

'I let my wife make all the decisions, and then I
go ahead and do what I want.'

'If I don't take any action, I don't have to face
any consequences, or at least I will experience no
negative consequences.'

Application of faulty laws equals or results in incorrect conclusions. A person's capacity becomes crippled in that area of life. There is less capacity to love, to feel, to serve, and to live a life of satisfaction. These people may consume their time with

---

[15] <u>The Power of Now</u> by Eckhart Toole, New World Library and Namaste Publishing

gossip and blame. Whenever we choose to blame, we are subconsciously saying, "I have rationalized my own conduct in the past, have missed the facts, and cannot see how to ever resolve it; and so I am directing blame at another person, group or institution. Certainly I am not to blame."

On the other hand if we always do what we know we should do, we will avoid the rationalization process, we will see things as they really are, and will be secure enough not to place blame. The truly secure person does not place blame. He has no need to do so.

I recently heard a story of the chief executive officer of a major corporation who presided over the company during a period when one of his top managers made a decision to invest an enormous sum of money in a business that later failed. When brought to task by the analysts on the issue later, rather than taking the easy path of blaming the executive who made the decision, the CEO said that he took full responsibility for the acquisition. He acknowledged it had been a mistake, and that the company would take precautions in the future based on the lessons it had learned from the experience. He never even mentioned blame. Can you see how this executive will have greater capacity in the future to expand his business and avoid repeating costly mistakes? What if he had placed blame? Would he recognize any need for improvement in his own performance? When we let blame resolve the matter, there is no further action to take.

Everyone wants to work for a boss who accepts responsibility and doesn't place blame on others. Soon the boss's subordinates will do all they can to make their boss look good. As a result, both the boss and employees are accomplishing greater things than ever before.

People who lack integrity also lack capacity and are therefore insecure. People who have integrity increase their capacity, trust and respect themselves, and have the security to move ahead with life.

Consider the case of the Kansas City Royals and their 2003 manager, Tony Pena. The 2003 season was expected to be an improbable season for the Royals due to three-fifths of their starting rotation plus three other players were on the disabled list. Yet, until the final days of the season, the Royals were in first place in their division. According to writers everywhere, the Kansas City Royals were successful because they had heart. According to all observers, the team got its heart from their new, effervescent manager, Pena, who turned the ragtag Royals into play-off contenders. They came within a whisker of becoming the first team to ever lose 100 games one season and make the play-offs the next.

In a "USA Today" article, Pena stated, "I always believed, but I had to get them to start believing."[16] The Royals arrived at their 2003 spring training with a reduced payroll of only $41 million and without their two best pitchers from the previous year. Tony Pena passed out T-shirts with the word "Believe!" embroidered in large blue letters. Underneath in Spanish was his signature statement, the translation to "Nosotros Creemos!" When the Royals closed the season 16-3, all of Kansas City started to believe as well.

If you don't have a dream, you cannot have a dream come true, was Pena's philosophy.

Pena, who is from the Dominican Republic, had an outstanding career in baseball himself, playing for eighteen years, catching in 1,945 games, being named to five all-star teams, winning four Gold Gloves and playing on four playoff teams (including the 1987 St. Louis Cardinals and 1995 Cleveland Indians World Series Clubs). For Pena, turning the Royals–with

---

[16] http://www.usatoday.com/sports/baseball/al/royals/2003-08-12-pena_html

a Wal Mart budget, compared with the Yankees' Saks Fifth Avenue spending–into a winning team seemed daunting at best.

Royals' pitcher Kris Wilson said, "He truly believed deep down in his heart that we could make the playoffs, challenge in our division, and even win our division."

Once the team started believing and realized he was serious, they agreed that Tony had something. He not only got the Royals to believe they could win, but his positive, encouraging, refreshing style created a tremendous team spirit that convinced everyone to work harder and win for manager, Pena. The team members integrated correct principles into their very beings. Every player started following the laws relating to physical conditioning, skills, and teamwork. They began to understand the link between believing, knowing what to do, and accomplishing. This resulted in a secure position for the team entering the playoffs.

Metal workers, bridge builders and airplane designers understand the critical need for integrity. The smallest weakness in the fabric or structure could cause a devastating result. The space shuttle Columbia had only a small breach near its wheel well that was caused by a falling piece of foam. Under the intense heat of re-entry into earth's atmosphere the entire ship broke in pieces. The same is true with people. It may have been a small breach in honesty, trust or discipline, but under the intense heat of life, it could unravel all the good we enjoy. A lack of integrity in a small area opens the door to ruin. Consider, for example, the case of another CEO who was arrested for insider trading. This CEO possessed many great traits. An immunologist turned entrepreneur, he developed a promising cancer drug, and engineered the biggest deal in the history of biotechnology. He was wealthy. He was one of Wall Street's brightest stars, but he had one crack in his integrity. Before he was imprisoned, he told his story of how he got into his mess.

Said he, "It certainly wasn't because I thought about it carefully ahead of time. I think I was arrogant enough at the time to believe that I could cut corners, not care about details that were going on, and not think about consequences."

Thinking that the stock was going down, he told his daughter to sell her shares.

"I was silly enough to believe that because it was such a de minimus amount of holding, I didn't think I was going to get caught at all."

He didn't have to sell the stock; he was a wealthy man. He had already made $60 million in the year 2000 and more than $70 million in 2001. He believed he was an honest person, but had one inconsistent behavior that cost him dearly. "I could sit there thinking I was the most honest CEO that ever lived. At the same time I could glibly do something and rationalize it because I cut a corner, since I didn't think I was going to get caught. One of my faults is that I refused to deal with everyday details that people have to deal with to make sure mistakes aren't made. I think, in that way, there may have been an arrogance where I didn't have to deal with details–that these details were meant for other people, not for me."

What has he learned from his problems? "Never break the law. Never lie to the U.S. government. I've learned not to be careless and not to be glib about things that I do. Because they can, these things can destroy all the good in one fell swoop. And, I'm sorry that these events had to take place for me to learn that. But, at least I've learned it."[17]

If you do not have integrity, you will never be secure—even if your rationalizations tell you that you are secure and that

---

[17] Interview on CBS "60 Minutes," October 6, 2003

you won't get caught. Most criminals sincerely believe that they will not get caught. Most do get caught.

When we can depend on the consistent integrity of others to perform according to their commitments, we are more secure. A wife whose husband honors his marital covenants is far more secure than the woman whose husband secretly abandons those commitments. We regularly hear of a betrayed wife discovering her husband's infidelity and of the heartache it causes. With the onset of HIV or other STD infections heartache can be only the beginning of her anguish. Such intense devastation can result from a husband who honored his commitment 99% of the time or who almost had integrity. The reversal of roles in this scenario, where the wife chooses to not honor her fidelity vows, can also add life-affecting problems for innocent husbands and children involved.

In the employment context, employers will pay a lot of money to employees who complete assigned tasks with promptness and provide feedback. A boss recognizes who he can count on to fulfill assignments. It is these "go to" employees who will represent the boss on committees, important tasks, and objectives. Employees who do not perform and report will soon find that their boss will not rely on them.

From the beginning of our lives, a fundamental question remains to be answered by each of us who runs the race of life. That question is: "Shall I falter or shall I finish? Shall I be dependable or undependable?" The answer to that question determines blessings of joy, love, and success–or not. Our security on the job depends on the answer to that question.

Security comes from knowing that you can depend on yourself and others to stick to a task, principle, or belief. Integrity is the key to security.

Stick to the Task, til it sticks to you;
Beginners are many, but enders are few;
Honor, power, place and praise
Will always come to the one who stays.
Stick to your task, til it sticks to you.
Bend at it, sweat at it, smile at it, too;
For out of the bend,
and the sweat and the smile
Will come life's victories after a while.[18]

---

[18] Author unknown

74

CHAPTER 5

YOUR PERSONAL CAPACITY CAN INCREASE

Recognition of weakness is the beginning of strength.

Whenever there is an unlimited supply of something, it cannot be referred to in finite terms. The one total freedom we all enjoy is the freedom of choice. In his compelling book, *Man's Search for Meaning*, Viktor Frankl describes the lessons he learned in a Nazi concentration camp. He learned that no one could take away his freedom to choose. That freedom is abundant and is in unlimited supply. Capacity is the same. It is the ability to reach out and exercise the freedom to choose based on known truths. It is only limited when we are blinded by our own rationalizations. It is unleashed infinitely when we act as we know we should act.

Capacity is like a muscle. The more we exercise it, the more ability or capacity we have to accomplish things. Like an unused muscle, when we ignore the things we know we should do, our capacity decreases until we can no longer do those things. With the lack of use, it becomes easier and easier to come up with excuses why something is not necessary, why we don't need it since we're already doing the best we can, and why the problem belongs to others instead of us. Eventually, the muscle will completely atrophy. Fortunately, there are shock treatments that we receive in life from time to time. They may come in the form of a job loss, a break-up, a break-down, an illness, or death of a loved one. While none of these things are pleasant, they may serve as wake-up calls. But why wait for a wake-up call?

As a young man, I was an avid water skier and had the physical ability to ski on one ski from a dock, a shore, or deep water. After a few years away from the lake, I was shocked to find that my muscles no longer had the capacity to start from deep water. That was a form of a wake-up call which I wished I had not waited for.

There is such abundance to be enjoyed in this life, such as physical abundance. Physical abundance is a schoolmaster to teach us of the greater abundance we can have in other areas of our lives. Modeling the path to physical abundance leads to abundance in other walks of life. We must recognize the facts about our own physical status (whether in terms of health or wealth), learn the applicable laws, practice the "should do" part of the laws, and reap the result. We can do the same in our spiritual lives, our emotional lives, our social lives, our financial lives, and in our roles as parents and leaders of industry and community. There is abundance to be found in each of these areas.

Not long ago, a young man died from a drug overdose. He began his course of life as an outstanding young man. As is the case with many young people, he greatly desired the respect and acceptance of others. He thought if he could gain the respect of others that would increase his self-respect. When seeking new friendships, it seems it's always easy to associate with the group of kids who seem to have little respect for themselves or for others, yet tend to bond together in their commonality. These individuals usually do not follow the traditional rules of society, but rather invent their own laws and regulations. This young man found many friends of this sort. They hung out together, they dressed differently, and they often felt it was them against the world. Some of them encouraged, even dared, one another to experiment with drugs.

The young man had been taught by his parents that it is harmful and wrong to take drugs and he knew the dangers. However, the dangers weren't immediately apparent to him as he observed his friends. Soon he rationalized the taking of drugs because his friends did, and they seemed to get relief and pleasure from doing so. In his rationalization, he still did not find any gained benefit—only pleasure in the moment and great remorse afterward. He could feel his real capacity and power diminishing as he continued to do what he knew he should not do. As his integrity was diminishing, so was his capacity.

He sought help and, though struggling, was overcoming the battle with drugs. Through the help and encouragement of his family— those who cared the most for him— he was making progress. He had been clean for two weeks. He was developing the wherewithal to resist the genuine urge to return to using drugs and gained greater power over his life. He was regaining his freedom.

Unfortunately, it was only in a moment of weakness that he succumbed. He was home alone and feeling discouraged. He rationalized that he would only take a small amount, but as he did, the desire to consume more grew stronger. He was found in his bed, dead of a drug overdose. Unfortunately, this story repeats itself every single day.

His death was a wake-up call for many of his friends to challenge their rationalizations. We all seem to use rationalizations to avoid truth. Hopefully, we will not need the wake-up calls of life to challenge those rationalizations, and we can begin doing, with integrity, what we know we should be doing.

Emotional blindness and rationalization are barriers to increasing capacity. Without those your capacity is as unlimited as your choices.

The Law of The Harvest

The old adage, "We reap what we sow," is sometimes referred to as the Law of the Harvest. It is a constructive analogy. The farmer cannot let himself be blinded by fantasies or false rationalizations. Crops will not raise themselves. They come as a result of the farmer knowing what to do and doing it. A novice farmer may not know all the principles that apply to raising crops. He may lose some along the way solely due to his naivety. His priority must be to learn what to do and to do it. It takes self-discipline getting up at 4:30 A.M. to tend to the livestock. It takes effort to stay on the combine all night long to obtain a timely wheat harvest. Knowledge is useless unless it is applied.

One example taken from agriculture follows: By using knowledge gained through inbreeding and hybridization, corn farmers have been able to increase their yields from approximately 85 bushels per acre in 1973 to over 142 bushels per acre in 2003.[19] This is a great example of where knowledge, along with the application of that knowledge, has led to increased capacity.

Several people contributed to or were interviewed for this

---

[19] http://www.usda.gov/nass/aggraphs/cornyld.html

book. Steve Albretch related a story about being raised in a farming community. He became acquainted with master farmers who had integrity—they were knowledgeable people and very disciplined. There were other people in the community who struggled to survive, either because they were not willing to learn what to do, or because they were not willing to do what they knew they should do. As with anything in life, there are laws of successful farming. Those who follow them consistently are much more successful than those who don't.

Steve related the following story: Two farmers lived side by side. Each started out with the same acreage of land and nearly the same number of cattle. Over a 15-year period, one of the farmers prospered. He followed the laws of good farming and good finances. He taught his children to be productive workers. The other farmer spent much of his time hanging out with friends who drank alcohol and partied. He did tend his farm, but only when it was convenient or absolutely necessary. He did many good things, but his actions were inconsistent. Eventually, he borrowed all that he was allowed, couldn't repay the debt, and lost the farm. It sounds like the story of the three little pigs. The moral to both stories is obvious.

The Law of the Harvest applies to all aspects of life. The harvest comes to those who know what to do and do it consistently. It doesn't matter whether we are farmers, educators, construction workers, businessmen or women, or homemakers. The law is the same. Those who indulge in rationalizations and self-deceptions will eventually "lose the farm." Sometimes they do not want to expend the effort that they know they should expend. Sometimes they fear that they won't realize the harvest after expending all the effort, and will be viewed as fools. Many attempt to hide their heads in the sand from the truth. After all, if one simply does not know the truth, one can hardly be blamed or ridiculed for not applying it.

"Who knew?" is all too often the shrug-off of our day. The only problem with this philosophy of denial is that the harvest never comes. Ignorance of the Law of the Harvest is the primary reason that AIDS continues to be on the increase in many of our populations, including high schools. "It just can't happen to me," is a rationalization that is resulting in death. It not only can happen to you, but there is a predictable statistic that it will happen to you if you engage in the deviant behavior.

Denial causes all types of problems. For example, even fraud perpetrators, while committing their fraudulent acts, deny that they are doing anything wrong. Rather, they rationalize that they are borrowing and will pay the money back or they justify their actions by thinking everyone does it. They will believe there is a big deal pending which will repay all the investors. Research has shown that there is a distinct set of five psychological reactions that people go through when they commit fraud. These reactions occur in a progressive order. Perhaps you know of someone who has been affected by fraud, even by a supposedly trusted friend or acquaintance—or, even worse, perhaps you have been personally touched by this increasingly occurring problem of our society.

Those reactions are:
        (1) denial
        (2) anger
        (3) rationalization
        (4) depression
        (5) acceptance

It has also been shown that these five reactions are common to almost any crisis we have in our lives. To recover our capacity and to have integrity in all we do, when we catch ourselves in any destructive behavior or when we are facing any personal challenge, we must move quickly through steps one to four and on to the acceptance stage. It is only when we accept reality that we can change.

The Law of the Harvest is really just another explanation of the relationship between integrity and capacity. If we follow the laws relating to the proper way to raise and harvest crops, we will have the capacity to increase our harvest. If we follow all of the laws pertaining to the successful operation of corporations, careers, families, finances etc., our individual and collective capacity will increase.

CHAPTER 6

CAPACITY IS BASED ON INTEGRATING CORRECT PRINCIPLES

Fear is a rationalization, a false association.

Desire is a fickle thing. Ask anyone on Madison Avenue. People can be led to think that they need a cigarette, a fancy car, a cheeseburger, a certain perfume, a certain style of clothing, an expensive watch, a larger home etc. Every year companies invest millions of dollars to advertise their wares in commercials that are designed to capture the hearts and appeal to the emotions of consumers. An average commercial ad aired during the Super Bowl costs $3.5 million for 30 seconds. This repetitive ad just 30 seconds in duration can have a statistically measured effect on the desires of the masses. That's why advertisers pay out huge sums of money. Not all ads are misleading, but when we are so easily misled by much advertising, how will we ever discover truth?

Advertisers know that if they can get you to make emotional associations in your mind, you will buy their products. Surely, consumers are more intelligent than that. In reality, however, it has nothing to do with intelligence. It is the way we are designed. Our brains learn both emotionally and intellectually. We learn by association–we associate visual and audio impressions both through an emotional process and through an intellectual process. Researchers tell us that there are separate physical systems in the structure of the brain to accommodate both types of learning. Studies done with children only one year old clearly demonstrate that emotional association is fully active far beyond the development of our rational minds. In the study, several children were exposed to a set of toys with which they played freely. Then they were exposed to a television actress who demonstrated varying emotional reactions to each of the toys. She reacted with expressions of shock and horror at some toys and expressions of fondness and acceptance to other toys. The children were then given the same toys to play with again, and their behavior mimicked the emotional reactions of the actress.

Improperly associating something to another thing that is not true is something humans can do and not even realize it. Our associations do not necessarily even need to correspond to the truth. This is especially true with emotional associations. Some people historically thought the world was flat. The world was always round, but for many years people were afraid to explore it, believing they would fall off the edge. Their association and belief was real, but the facts they associated with it were not. Their association kept them from action. It held them back. It limited their capacity for great discovery and wealth. Blindness to correct principles limits capacity.

Conversely, proper associations can also propel us forward to action. They can do this for better or for worse. This is the principle that underlies the multi-billion dollar advertising industry. Advertisers believe that if they can get you to associate a positive feeling with their product, such as a feeling of pleasure or satisfaction, that you will eventually purchase their product in pursuit of that feeling. It works! It has been statistically proven. The industry accurately measures the effect of a good advertisement by the corresponding increase in sales.

However, the associations people make with advertised products are not always real. It is our understanding that cigarettes do not taste good, yet many people would dispute that because they associate smoking cigarettes with a clever and long standing advertisement that said: "___ tastes good like a cigarette ___."[20]

Most of us who lived through the advertising campaign, can't even read the foregoing sentence without mentally filling in the blanks. So what are the associations that advertisers want us to make? They want us either to associate a fear of some type of pain or humiliation with not using their product, or to develop an association for a feeling of love, acceptance, or respect with the use of their product. They are attacking our emotional learning system. If we are going to have integrity, we must learn to recognize how and why our emotional associations affect us, and whether or not they are real and true.

Fear of pain

The two things that motivate most of us to action in life can be described either as pain and pleasure, or as penalty and reward. Law enforcement is designed around the principle

---

[20] Winston . . . Should.

that the fear of punishment can prevent people from breaking the law. At a fundamental level we need to believe that the reward or pleasure that will result from our actions will be more satisfying than the penalty or pain our actions may cause us. Many people do not accomplish the things they purport to desire in life because they fail to take action. They fail to take action because they are fearful that the price they will have to pay by taking action will be too painful for them. We all tend to stay within our comfort zone. Why? Because we are comfortable! It is pleasurable for us to feel comfortable. We like it. We seek it. Why would we give up our comfort?

That is a key question we should ask ourselves in life. It is difficult, however, to clearly understand the answer. For instance, most people don't really understand what it would be like to live in a mansion. Oh, when we were children we could imagine doing so, even living in a castle. As we grow older, we make fewer and fewer attempts to envision ourselves living in a mansion or castle. Why? We become fearful! After being introduced to the work world and learning what kind of effort goes into making a dollar, we begin to envision the pain and effort associated with making enough money to purchase and maintain a mansion. Our minds make associations. These associations are not always true, but we still make them. We rapidly come to rationalize that the price to pay is too high, the pain would be too great, and we close off our minds to the possibility. Of course, this is just an example. No eternal truth hinges on whether we are living in a mansion, but the pain and pleasure associated with truly important things are usually even harder to clearly visualize in our conscious minds.

Later in the book, we will discuss how our associations with pain limit our capacity to be productive. For now, we want to be clear that fear of pain is a factor everyone deals with.

Ultimately, we choose to take action because our minds associate a positive relative value between our goals and the price we must pay to achieve our goals. Without this positive relative value, we simply wouldn't act.

Love is an example of the mental association of a positive relative value. Our minds usually associate great pleasure to our future association with the person who is the object of our love. We tend to look at our intended through rose-colored glasses, ignoring flaws or defects. It is this positive mental value that allows us to move towards marriage, make a life-long commitment, and take action.

Fear of intellectual ridicule

How is it that most of us are somehow taught to fear criticism or ridicule? You would think we would all welcome criticism as feedback in order to evaluate ourselves in our self-improvement process. Why do so few people ask questions or make comments in public meetings? Is it that they have nothing to say or is it that they are afraid to speak for fear of ridicule or embarrassment?

Most of our fears are learned. We were not born with them. The emotional scars we have are a result of our interactions with others—either in our homes, or after leaving our safe homes and going to elementary school and beyond. They are associations between actions and feelings. We made these associations when we were very young and they are extremely powerful, still affecting our behavior as adults. They were lessons taught to the emotional side of the brain.

Many students purposely hold back from the learning process and from asserting themselves because they fear ridicule.

They know they could do better if they put in the hours of study and class presentation, but they do not put in the effort. They do not want to feel that they did their best and came up short. It would be too painful. Other students might tease them about their performance after working as hard as they could. It would make them feel intellectually inferior.

By holding back they can always say, "Hey, I didn't even try." This process can repeat itself throughout life at many different levels. It is a basic rationalization that allows us to cope with not really applying the principles we know to be correct.

Similar shortcuts and rationalizations motivate people to be dishonest. As an example, consider Susan Jones (actual case, name changed). She had worked at the same company for over 32 years. Her integrity had never been questioned. At age 63, she became a grandmother and she knew she didn't make enough money to provide what she wanted to give her grandchildren. So she started stealing (a shortcut) to get the money she felt she needed to be a good grandmother. As she spent money on her grandchildren, the more she wanted to spend on them and on everything else! Before long, she became a spend-a-holic, buying everything she could get her hands on for her two grandchildren. She even became addicted to the Home Shopping Network, a cable television channel. During the three years prior to her retirement, Susan stole over $650,000 from her employer. When caught, she was sentenced and served one year in prison. Also, she deeded everything she and owned over to her former employer—in an attempt to pay the employer back. By giving her employer her home, her retirement account, and her cars, she repaid approximately $400,000 of the $650,000 stolen. She also entered into a restitution agreement to pay back the remaining $250,000 she still owed, although in reality her monthly payments wouldn't even cover the interest on the $250,000 she still owed. Since she had not paid income taxes on the $250,000 of fraudulent income, the IRS required her to make monthly tax payments after she got out of prison. She could have worked harder and been wiser in her purchases, but she rationalized her shortcuts. Now, she has less than nothing.

Fear of emotional embarrassment

There is no hurt so deep as the hurt we associate with emotional embarrassment. Most of us are extremely careful about what we share at an emotional level. Without a relationship of trust and love, we seldom lay our feelings on the line. It is too easy for others to hurt our feelings and leave us in a state of emotional pain. Many of us hesitate to reveal our admiration or affection, because if we are rejected, the pain at an emotional level is almost too much to bear. We will do almost anything to avoid emotional pain. Those most fearful of emotional pain sometimes completely cloak or deny their emotions.

School-aged children can be the most emotionally cruel of all people despite their innocence. Children make their associations without evaluation. Often what hurts the most is their accuracy—at least at the most basic level. The imperfections they point out are often true, but the meanings they attach to them are often irrational. If someone has a big nose, a different color of skin, a blemish, or even a birth defect, the other kids are quick to notice and point it out to all. Unfortunately, at this age they often ridicule. While the observation might be true, the emotional reaction is false. Nevertheless, there are many teenagers and adults who suffer immensely from such things as thinking their nose is too large or their complexion is bad. It greatly limits them and their willingness to venture out socially, emotionally, spiritually, and physically.

To understand how children suffer from ridicule, consider the story of Amy Jo Hagadorn. A number of years ago, in Fort Wayne, Indiana, WILT radio station sponsored a Christmas Wish Contest. The contest was only open to children 12 years of age and under. When the contest was announced, the station received many letters from children of that age group, but one particular letter stood out among the others. A young girl named Amy wrote the following letter:

> *Dear Santa Claus:*
>
> *My name is Amy. I am 9 years old. I have a problem at school. Can you help me, Santa? Kids laugh at me because of the way I walk and run and talk. I have cerebral palsy. I just want one day where no one laughs at me or makes fun of me.*
>
> *Love, Amy*

The station manager read the narrowed down pile created by his employees. He realized that cerebral palsy, like other handicapping diseases, could be misunderstood and confusing to Amy's schoolmates who didn't understand her disability. He decided the people of Fort Wayne should hear about this special third-grader and her unusual wish. He called up the local newspaper, The News Sentinel. The following day, a picture of Amy and her special letter to Santa was printed. The story was a popular read, and other newspapers and radio and television stations throughout the United States reported the story of this little girl in Fort Wayne, Indiana, and her tender request for just one thing–one day without teasing. The city mayor proclaimed December 21st as *Amy Jo Hagadorn Day* in Fort Wayne declaring that Amy had taught everyone a lesson.

Fear of loneliness

One of the most potent fears that advertisers play on is the fear of loneliness. There are many things we believe we can do to avoid loneliness. We can apply make-up, we can diet and become thinner, we can dress in the latest style, we can socialize in a harmful way, we can drive a fancy car, etc. Are any of these things really related to having friends? Or are they just the result of irrational associations that advertisers have created in our minds through frequent exposure to symbol association?

In reality, friendship depends on the love, trust, service, empathy, support, and kindness we show others much more than it does on what we wear or drink. We actually feel less lonely when we are serving others, and yet most of us hold back from serving others because our selfish associations overpower our selfless associations.

Fear of not being understood

One of our most basic needs is to feel understood. Feeling that we are not understood creates a feeling of loneliness. Think how frustrating it would be if you could never be understood! At the basic level we need to be understood. Often we don't speak up when we should because of this fear. It is said that a woman's most basic social need is the need to feel understood. The psychological need to be understood is the equivalent of the physiological need for air!

In his book, *Men are From Mars, Women are from Venus*, John Gray states that men get their sense of self from achievement. According to Gray, men tend to be task-oriented and self-reliant. Women, on the other hand, get their sense of self from relationships. Where men are task-oriented, women are relational-oriented. Their connections to other people are the most important thing to them. Instead of prizing self-reliance, they tend to be interdependent, enjoying the connectedness to other people, especially other women. In those relationships, being understood is extremely important to women.

It's not only women who need to be understood. A few years ago, a research organization asked several thousand people, "What are the most serious faults of executives in dealing with their associates and subordinates?"

The results were as follows:

15%	Bias and letting emotions rule
15%	Indecision
17%	Failure to delegate authority
17%	Arrogance
17%	Arbitrariness
19%	Lack of frankness and sincerity
21%	Miscellaneous; including lack of courtesy, sarcasm, jealousy, nervousness, and loss of temper
24%	Lack of leadership
34%	Failure to size up employees correctly
36%	Failure to show appreciation or give credit
68%	Failure to see the other person's point-of-view

The fault cited most often, as the survey shows, was failure to see the other person's point-of-view or to understand the other person. It was mentioned nearly twice as often as the next most common problem.

Stated another way, the strength most valued in the workplace is the ability to understand others. That strength rates high in all relationships. We don't always need others in our life to agree with us, but we do need to feel heard and understood. In fact, feeling understood may well be one of our greatest emotional needs. Without it, we can feel disheartened; we believe we don't matter, and we find ourselves increasingly unhappy and lonely.

Grade school children demonstrate this important human need to be heard and understood. One writer tells about a group of children who seldom talked about personal problems with their teachers or the school principal for fear of the consequences. In which of the adults at school were the children confiding most often? They found a person who would listen without judging. He was someone who was safe, someone who would understand. He was he school custodian!

Author Og Mandino gives us this challenge: "Beginning today, treat everyone you meet as if they were going to be dead by midnight. Extend to them all the care, kindness, and understanding you can muster, and do it with no thought of any reward. Your life will never be the same again."[21]

It's a universal principle: When we habitually decide to be understanding, we soon feel more understood. When we practice this principle, our lives are never the same again.

---

[21]http://thinkexist.com/quotation/beginning_today_treat_everyone_you_meet_as_if/14362.html

Fear of incompetence or failure

The fear of incompetence is related to the fear of ridicule and the fear of embarrassment. No one wants to do something incompetently. Some people would rather not take on a project than to do it poorly. Can you see how this fear can stop us from achieving?

Consider this actual example. Anyone who wants to go to graduate school in business in the United States takes a competency-based examination called the Graduate Management Aptitude Test (GMAT). The fee for taking the exam is $250, and even more if the applicant wants results to be sent to more than five business schools. It is an exam that one can repeat as many times as he or she wants. Schools usually only consider your highest score. A certain young man studied hard to prepare for the test. On testing day, he approached the testing center feeling somewhat confident. As he was taking the test, he started worrying that his score was going to be too low and that he would suffer embarrassment among his family and friends. Just as he was ready to finish and wait for the computer to assess his test score, he suddenly pushed the escape key and exited the examination. In this case, where there was really no penalty for getting a low score, this young man chose to exit the examination rather than suffer the *potential* embarrassment of obtaining a low score. His fear stopped him from doing—even when the rewards from getting a score far outweighed any penalty he would have incurred.

**Fears are rationalizations
that can be overcome by integrity.**

All of our fears have a basis in the irrational. They are usually false associations. We can imagine the bogey man in the attic quite vividly. There was a young girl who truly believed that there was a man living in her attic. People had told her scary stories about such things, and she was convinced of hearing noises in the attic on a regular basis. She spent a lot of her time thinking about the man in her attic. She would tell her young cousins about it. One day she thought she saw him staring at her from the attic window. She was terrified. Neither she nor her cousins would go near the attic door. They imagined this fear so clearly, and made such a clear association that they were afraid to take action due to the false association of pain. They imagined themselves being dragged into the attic and being never found. Their fears consumed them.

Helen Keller once said, "There is statistically no difference in the safety of those who hold back and those who take bold action."

This is because the fears that cause most people to hold back are almost always based on false associations of pain. They become hypnotic specters of unpleasantness that never materialize for those that ignore them and choose to act.

Advertising is a game of false associations regarding fear or pain. Do people really want the products they consume? The acquisition of consumer goods often leaves us feeling empty inside, because the products fail to deliver the emotional satisfaction their advertisements promise. It is a bait and switch—a mental association game that draws on powerful personal motivations to influence behavior. These advertisements often prey upon the overweight, the depressed, and the impotent.

How does advertising influence our beliefs about what we want? Modern culture relentlessly suggests to us that acceptance, security, and pleasure are related to our allegiance to one brand image over another. The cumulative effect of this advertising bombardment is a modern society that believes happiness is linked to beauty, wealth, and fame.

Are these things really associated or have our minds merely become convinced that they are associated? Suppose they are not. Consider the possibility of beautiful people who never experience love. Imagine the prospect of wealthy people who are never really accepted or talented people who are not well-respected. What if there are people with many possessions, who cannot be trusted and are not happy?

Much of what we are taught on television and in our culture is not rooted in correct principles. It is the same association game that the advertisers play to get us to buy products. Our impressionable minds tend to believe that by emulating the images we see, we can get happiness, security, and pleasure. The television series "Friends" was delightfully funny, well-acted by beautiful people, and well-written. So many young people have associated the life style of "Friends" with happiness and acceptance. They don't realize that the series is a fantasy world. The lifestyle and consequences portrayed on that program would never flow from many of the life choices of these fictional characters.

**Developing increased personal capacity
can be achieved by the integration
of correct principles into our lives.**

There is a big lie that has perpetrated our society, which can be labeled *Individual Reality.* The premise of this concept is that reality is different for each individual. It has been expressed in these terms: "It doesn't really matter what set of principles you select to live your life by—it just matters that you select a set of principles to govern your life. That way you will know how to act and will have consistency from day to day." This philosophy holds that correct principles do not exist and that each individual's principles are relative to that individual.

Though each individual might experience reality in a different way, there is only one reality. There is a set of governing laws throughout all space and time. Many, if not most, of these laws are not fully discovered or understood. However, many are! Though the operation of the law of gravity is not fully understood, the effects are. People might experience the law of gravity differently, yet the law is the same and everyone must integrate it into their life at the very beginning of our earthly existence. Gravity is a true, or correct, principle.

Integrity has to do with the completeness with which we incorporate the correct principles that we become aware of throughout our lives. It is the absence of that guilt associated with not doing what we know to do. It is the absence of false associations or rationalizations. It may take years of experience and adjustment for us to overcome our false associations and discover all of the correct principles there are to discover. Although many people have discovered these principles for themselves, incorporated them into their lives, and written about them for our benefit, each of us must learn these principles on our own.

Benjamin Franklin selected thirteen virtues to work on every day. They are as follows:

- Temperance/Moderation: restraint, self-control
- Tranquility/Silence: peaceful, calmness, stillness
- Order: organization, tidiness
- Resolution: decisive, tenacity, perseverance
- Frugality: thriftiness, prudence,
- Industry: diligence, productiveness, conscientiousness
- Sincerity: genuineness, honesty, authenticity
- Justice: fairness, impartiality, integrity
- Cleanliness: hygiene, sanitation
- Chastity: pureness, clean within
- Humility: modesty, unassuming nature

It was through integrating these virtues that Benjamin Franklin became the great individual that he was. The same can be true for us. By integrating virtues we will not only obtain security, self worth, and self-respect, but we will become better people. Too often, because we are continually bombarded by images of the unchaste, of the dishonest, of the unkind in our movies and television shows, many of us tend to emulate these untoward traits. We do so with the false assumption that there is value to be found there. We do it with the false assumption that we can find happiness in wrong-doing. This is never the case.

As an illustration of how images and illusions can cause deviant behavior, consider the case of the Washington area snipers, John Allen Muhammad and John Lee Malvo. Video games have been brought up as a possible motive for the sniper suspects. According to an article in the Washington, D.C. area newspaper, the investigators believed that several violent video games, such as "Grand Theft Auto," were a likely motive behind the sniper attacks. Many crimes appear to have been perpetrated by individuals who patterned their criminal acts after movies they had seen, video games they had played, or music they had heard. Usually this is done under the false belief that rewards of fame or wealth would ensue in some meaningful way. Some role-playing Internet or purchased games take countless people from living real lives to spending all their waking hours as a hero or heroine in a mere game, where their character overtakes their real selves, and they neglect or even ignore their own needs or the needs of their families.

Often these same false associations and rationalizations lead people to be dishonest as well. Experts who study dishonesty, and especially fraud, often refer to something called the fraud triangle. The fraud triangle indicates that there are three key elements common to all frauds. These three elements are: (1) a perceived pressure, (2) a perceived opportunity, and (3) some way to rationalize the fraud as being acceptable.

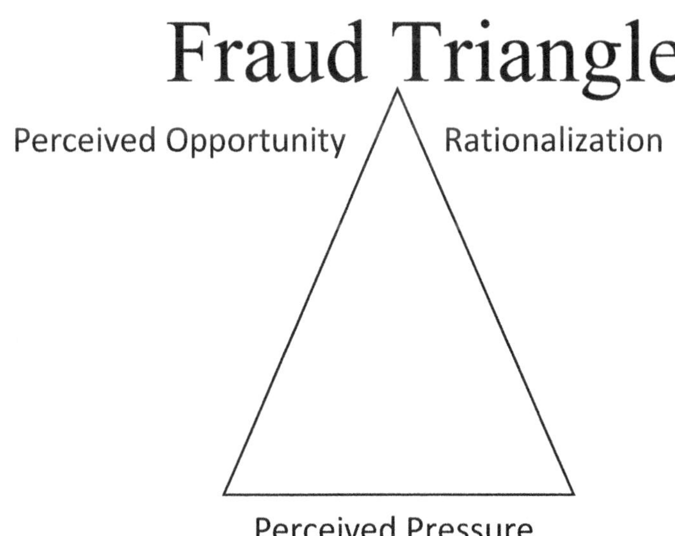

The pressures and opportunities do not have to be real. Rather they only need to be assumed or perceived pressures and opportunities.

You may look at a fraud perpetrator and express, "You didn't have to steal; you didn't have any pressures."

Yet we find it doesn't really matter what you think–only what the perpetrator thinks and how he has associated his need with an emotional pressure. Similarly, a person who embezzles may not have actual opportunities, only perceived opportunities.

You may think, for instance, 'How stupid was that?' when considering the actions of the perpetrator. 'Didn't they know they would be caught?' Again, reality doesn't really have an impact on the offender–it is enough to believe they could get away with it.

Every fraud perpetrator faces some kind of perceived pressure. Most perceived pressures involve financial need, although non-financial pressures, such as the need to report results better than actual performance to avoid embarrassment, frustration with work pressures, or even a challenge to beat the system can motivate fraud.

Consider the case of another high level executive, who was convicted in 2005 of crimes related to his receipt of $81 million in purportedly unauthorized bonuses, the purchase of art for $15 million, and payment by his company of a $20 million investment banking fee to a former director. The former CEO had lived a lavish lifestyle, and used company funds to pay for much of it, including a reported $15,000 dog umbrella. But perhaps the most extravagant was a $2.1 million, ancient Roman-theme party he held for his wife on a small island off the coast of Italy. What follows is a memo, part of a Securities and Exchange Commission investigation, that details plans for the birthday bash. Following is the invitation to said bash with some of the vulgarities excluded:

Subject: Birthday Bash — June 14, 2001

Guests arrive at the club starting at 7:15 p.m. The van pulls up to the main entrance. Two gladiators are standing next to the door, one opens the door, the other helps the guests. We have a lion or horse with a chariot for the shock value.

The guests proceed through the two rooms. We have gladiators standing guard every couple feet and they are lining the way. The guests come into the pool area, the band is playing, they are dressed in elegant chic. Big ice sculpture of David, lots of shellfish and caviar at his feet. A waiter is pouring Stoli vodka into his back so it comes out his [privates] into a crystal glass.

Waiters are passing cocktails in chalices. They are dressed in linen togas with fig wreath on head. A full bar with fabulous linens.

The pool has floating candles and flowers. We have rented fig trees with tiny lights everywhere to fill some space, 8:30 the waiters instruct that dinner is served. We all walk up to the loggia. The tables are all family style with the main table in front.

The tables have incredible linens with chalices as wineglasses. The food is brought out course by course, family style, lots of wine, and it's starting to get dark. Everyone is nicely buzzed, [the CEO] gets up and has a toast for [his wife].

Everyone is jumping from table to table. [The band] has continued to play light music through dinner. They kick it up a bit.

We start the show of pictures on the screen, great background music in sync with the slides. At the end, Elvis is on the screen wishing the wife a Happy Birthday and apologizing that he could not make it.

It starts to fade and Elvis is [actually] onstage and starts singing happy birthday with the Swingdogs. A huge cake is brought out with the waiters in togas singing and holding the cake up for all to see.

The cake explodes, Elvis kicks it in full throttle. Waiters are passing wine, after dinner drinks, and there is dancing. 11:30 light show starts. HBK [Happy Birthday and wife's name] is displayed on mountain, fireworks coming from both ends of the golf course in sync with music. Swingdogs start up and the night is young.

Do you believe this executive had a real pressure to throw that lavish of a party with company funds for his wife? Doubtful! Rather, he associated the party with a fun time and had a perceived pressure to do something incredible. Similarly, he associated his being CEO of the company as allowing him the opportunity to spend company money however he wanted to, even if it wasn't appropriate. This kind of emotional thinking led him to serve 8 ¼ - 24 years in a New York correctional facility. Was it worth it?

Perceived pressure, perceived opportunity, and rationalization are common to every fraud. Whether the fraud is one that benefits the perpetrators directly, such as employee fraud, or one that benefits the perpetrator's organization, such as management fraud, the three elements are always present. In the case of management fraud, for example, executives often perceive that they must make earnings look better in order to meet debt covenants. Perhaps they will perceive an opportunity in the form of a weak audit committee, and they rationalize that they will only cook the books to get over a temporary slump. In the perpetrator's mind, there is always a perception that circumstances will change allowing the fraud to be rectified or justified.

Whether it is emotional association, rationalization, or ignorance of correct principles, we often have a hard time self-diagnosing our situation and why we are not taking appropriate action to achieve positive results. In many cases, it is essential to have a coach or a mentor to help us realize our false association or belief. Until we wake up to our situation, it is impossible to take the actions we need to take and to get the results we really want. The job of the mentor or coach is to lift our vision, help us identify what we really want, to see the obstacles that stand in our way, to teach us the formula for achieving the results, and to hold us accountable for taking the actions we need to take.

Everyone needs a coach! One might find a coach in a friend, family member, peer, co-worker, or perhaps a more professional one is needed, such as a business leader or a professional in various fields of service.

Coaching is one of the growing industries in the United States. As more and more people realize that they need help in identifying weaknesses (the beginning of strength), identifying actions, and becoming accountable, they will seek out a coach.

I have designed an Integrity Coaching Program to provide assistance to anyone that wants to develop greater capacity in their lives or organizations. (See reference at end of book).

CHAPTER 7

BECOMING CLEAR
ON WHAT YOU WANT

Overcoming Fear and
the Power of Imagination

Because the mind can believe an association that it intellectually knows is not true, it is extremely important that we gain a clear vision of what we want and what is required to get it. It sounds so easy.

If it really were that easy, the mind association game wouldn't work. Advertisers would have us believe that drinking beer is associated with attracting sexy women or tall, dark, handsome men. In fact, the opposite is more likely to be true. There are several false associations our minds make in connection with advertising. There is no long-lasting benefit to scantily-clad women as immodesty will not attract men of character. Beer is not a means of attracting the opposite sex. Yet, our minds develop the visual images and we make the subconscious emotional association. Powerful influences are at work. Our vision is obscured by our visualizations and emotional associations.

Organizations work hard to create mind associations through their advertising campaigns. They know they will be effective and that we will purchase their products. Because of that, they spend more than $12 billion a year on marketing. Each of us sees between 20,000 and 40,000 ads a year. Whether we realize it or not, seeing these ads affects and influences our purchasing decisions and actions.

Advertisers are adept at getting us to buy things even when we don't have a good reason or need them. It is an emotional game of association. Here's what a famous advertising executive once said about how companies try to get kids to buy: "Advertising at its best is making people feel that without their product you're a loser. Kids are very sensitive to that. If you tell them to buy something, they are resistant. But if you tell them they'll be a dork if they don't, you've got their attention."

To illustrate how effective advertisers are, see how easily it is for you to finish some long-standing ad slogans or identify the product being pitched:

<u>POPULAR ADVERTISING SLOGANS</u>

1. ____ is the place for the helpful hardware man.
2. Plop, plop, fizz, fizz, oh what a relief it is!
3. You're in good hands with ____________.
4. Don't leave home without it.
5. Reach out and touch someone!
6. Wassssuuuuuppp?
7. Have it your way!
8. M'm, M'm, Good!
9. Please don't squeeze the ___________.
10. It's the real thing.
11. Aren't you glad you use ______? Don't you wish everyone did?

12. Double your pleasure, double your fun.
13. It keeps going and going and going . . .
14. When it absolutely, positively, has to be there overnight.
15. A day without orange juice is like a day without sunshine.
16. We bring good things to life.
17. In the valley of the Jolly, "Ho, ho, ho, _________ __________."
18. No more tears.
19. Snap! Crackle! Pop!
20. Finger-licking good.
21. Betcha can't eat just one!
22. The chocolate melts in your mouth–not in your hands.
23. You deserve a break today.
24. Our repairmen are the loneliest guys in town.
25. Good to the last drop!
26. Just do it.
27. When it rains, it pours.
28. I wish I was an _____ ______ _______!
29. Nothing says lovin' like something from the oven.
30. _______, the San Francisco treat.
31. How do you spell relief?
32. Nobody doesn't like ______ ________.
33. Fly the friendly skies of __________.
34. A mind is a terrible thing to waste.
35. Be all that you can be.
36. It's everywhere you want to be.
37. Where's the beef?
38. Breakfast of Champions.
39. Let your fingers do the walking.

Note: For product answer key, see Appendix A

Did you know that research suggests children starting at the age of three remember and repeat these slogans? There are complicated mechanisms in our minds. The mind association game works. Our mind believes whatever we can clearly visualize. This important feature of the mind can also work to our advantage.

W. Clement Stone put it this way, "Whatever the mind of man can conceive and believe—it can achieve."

We also have a protective device that closes the shutters in our mind to prevent us from visualizing things we associate with an imbalance of pain, embarrassment, or betrayal. The closing of this shutter limits our capacity, our vision, and our clarity. Likewise, the shutter opens to view anything that we associate with success and happiness. It works this way whether or not the association is real. When we perceive personal or emotional risk, our capacity is limited. We just don't see ourselves taking charge of the issues or leading the organization. We don't see ourselves at the podium, speaking out on serious issues of our day. We just don't see ourselves running a restaurant chain, owning our own home, working in a management position, writing a book, making a movie, or being a mother or a committed husband etc. And it is true! Once the shutters close, we just can't see clearly what we want. We can't become what we want. Our capacity is limited. We are damned in the sense that water is held back by the structure of the dam. What we say we want is often not what we truly want. A better indicator of what we want is what we have. That is what we truly want.

Successful leaders know there are at least four steps to effectively open these shutters of our minds and get things accomplished. Since each of us is a leader in some aspect, whether we desire to be or not, we should familiarize ourselves with these four steps.

• First, leaders must have a vision of what needs to be accomplished.

• Second, leaders must put in place processes that will help them accomplish their vision.

• Third, leaders must identify what the biggest risks are for not completing the process or realizing the vision, and put risk-mitigating measures in place.

• Fourth, leaders must communicate effectively to others who are affected by their leadership.

Some of us don't think we can be leaders because we don't know how to visualize. Others of us don't believe we can communicate effectively. The first step in seeing ourselves as successful leaders is to understand what leadership means and then figuring out how to accomplish these four steps. It's not that some people are innately leaders and others aren't. It's that some learn to do whatever it takes to realize a goal.

Consider the political path of Abraham Lincoln's road to the White House. When he was 7 years of age, his family was forced out of their home. He had to work to support them. At age 9, he lost his mother. When he was 22, his business failed. At age 23, he ran for the Illinois State Legislature. He finished eighth in a race that had only 13 candidates. He not only lost the political race, but he also lost his job. He wanted to go to law school, but was not admitted. At age 24, he ran for the state legislature again, and this time, he won! A year later, he was engaged to be married; his fiance died, and his heart was so saddened he had a nervous breakdown and was in bed for six months. When he was 29 and a member of the Illinois House of

Representatives, Lincoln lost a battle for the Speaker of the House. When he was 34, he ran for Congress and lost. At age 37, Lincoln ran for Congress again and won! At age 39, he ran for re-election to Congress and lost. When he was 45, he sought the vice-presidential nomination at the party's national convention and received less than 100 votes, losing once more. At age 49, Lincoln again ran for the U.S. Senate, and yet another time, he lost. Finally, when he was 51, he was elected as the 16th President of the United States. Along the way, Lincoln experienced some victories, but his failures far outnumbered his wins He could have given up on his dreams; he could have quit many times, but he wouldn't and he didn't. Nothing would deter this man.

If we are to overcome the bombardment of false associations that we confront every day, it will require developing a strong integrity muscle. It is interesting that Benjamin Franklin explained his virtue of resolution, much like our definition of integrity. He said that we should "resolve to perform what we ought, and perform without fail what we resolve."

He understood that when we decide to not do the things we know that we should do, we will begin to rationalize and develop false associations, and have a distorted view of reality. With a distorted and false view of reality, we cannot take actions that will be effective or efficient. Thereby we lose capacity. We must be able to see things as they really are in order to act with respect to them in any effective manner. This is applicable to corporations, families, and individuals.

Integrity and capacity are highly interrelated. Capacity is based on the integration of correct principles. The failure to act, to do what we know we should do, results in rationalizations that paralyze us from taking further action. In a spiritual parlance (manner of speaking), when we sin (therefore to him that knoweth to do good, and doeth it not) we are damned (unable to take further effective action).

As human beings, the only creatures on the earth with the ability to act rationally, we have unlimited capacity. Animals do not make rational choices based on principles as we do. They are confined to act within their instincts and follow the same patterns year in and year out. Inanimate objects must be acted upon and have no ability to act. We alone have the power to act. We can invent. We have dramatically changed the way we live over the past one hundred years and throughout history. We have the capacity for self-improvement. Only our false associations and fears limit us.

Our fears close off the shutters in our minds and prevent us from seeing what we can become. They prevent us from even grasping the success that we can have in any part of life, whether it be financial, emotional, social, political, occupational, physical, or spiritual. Shutters prevent us from seeing ourselves as we really are or as we can become, and prevent us from seeing that there are correct principles—laws that, if obeyed, will result in increased capacity. So how do we overcome our fears? How do we put aside our false associations? How do we incorporate correct principles into our lives?

Visualize success to achieve success.

You must not only want success, but you must create it. One of the ways to create success is to act with the self-confidence of a successful person. If you know the laws for achieving any given result, it will raise the level of your self-confidence. If you visualize yourself applying the laws and achieving the result, it will help you to act.

Whatever your specific goal is, picture the scenario and see yourself acting successfully. For instance, if your goal is to get venture capital for your company, imagine yourself presenting your business plan to a group of potential venture capitalists.   Picture yourself as confident, relaxed, and knowledgeable. Go through the pitch in your head. See and hear your audience asking questions and answer them. Picture a successful outcome, such as, in this case, the audience wanting to invest in your company. When you've finished running through this visualizing success exercise, you'll feel your confidence rising and feel more relaxed. Perform this exercise every day, as many times as possible before the actual event. What will happen is that the image can become the reality. By imagining yourself taking the necessary actions to achieve success, you will be able to achieve success. When it comes time to make the presentation, you will feel confident, relaxed, and knowledgeable—because you've already done it so many times prior in your mind, and you now have a much better chance at a favorable outcome. Achieving business success isn't just a matter of preparing plans and financial reports; you also need to prepare yourself to act and be successful. Visualizing success beforehand will help you do that. [22]

One CEO, watching the famous speech delivered by George C. Scott in the movie, "Patton," visualized himself making that speech prior to every major speech he delivered.

The first step in developing greater personal capacity is to see clearly the image of what you want to become and to realize that the path is clear of the obstacles you fear. The only way to do this is to learn and rely on the correct principles or laws upon which the results you desire are based. Once you know the correct principles you can choose to have confidence that they will lead to the intended result. The integrity building process is designed to help you achieve these objectives.

There is an observable process of learning in life.

[22] Ward, Susan. "Increase Your Business Success by Visualizing Success," http://sbinfocanada.about.com/cs/management/qt/visualizesuccess.html

Think about a child who is learning to walk. The process requires weeks of just trying to stand holding onto something. Then it takes some adventurous letting go and falling down. Eventually, with a little coaxing and feeling of security from a parent, the child takes the first step. There will be several more falls, but eventually walking will become second nature.

You must plan on failure in order to achieve your goals. Children probably don't even think about not falling down—they expect to fall down and can deal with it. They don't give up, but keep trying to walk. They observe people all around them walking. Eventually, they can imagine themselves walking and begin to make attempts. Soon they are successful and hardly ever fall down.

Many adults completely give up on their financial, marriage, family, career, health, or social goals because they cannot visualize themselves being responsible to take actions to achieve those goals. They can only see the hazards and the risks. They would rather put their entire future in the hands of someone else. It would be like a child who couldn't visualize himself walking, so rather than walking, he would rely on his parents to carry him from room to room. Many times, we act like this child in our financial, emotional, social, spiritual, physical and intellectual spheres.

Another process that can be instructive is the process of learning to play the piano. Anyone can learn at any age if they are willing to follow the process. It begins with a desire and a vision. Often an instructor is sought out. A plan is developed which involves making a commitment to practice for a certain amount of time each day. If the plan is followed, the result follows. Many people never attempt to learn to play the piano, although the process is simple and well-known. They are inhibited by their self-image. "Oh, I am just not the musical type," they might say. The truth is that they are afraid. Maybe they are fearful of embarrassment, ridicule, failure, or commitment. Perhaps they simply do not believe the process will work for them. When the piano player is able to see or visualize the image of what he or she can become, the mind will do everything possible to help him or her achieve the goal.

John Greenleaf Whittier said: "For all sad words of tongue or pen, the saddest are these: It might have been!"[23]

How can we open up the shutters of our vision to see what we can become? We spoke earlier of how the mind can believe repetitive visual associations, even when it logically knows that they are not true. The opposite phenomenon is also observable. Sometimes our mind refuses to make certain associations, even when it knows they are true. For example, many people do not associate caloric intake with being overweight, even though they know the scientific laws associated with it. Many people do not associate thrift with financial security.

Capacity Vision

The process of capacity vision is a tool we can use in developing integrity. Capacity vision is the view of what we can become in any area of our lives based on the integration of correct principles. It is a view of what our lives could be like if our dim vision, unbelief, or false associations did not limit us. Since the mind can easily make associations based on commercial visualized affirmations of things that are not associated, just think how much more powerful affirmations can be for visualizing what really can be, what really is associated. Correct principles are, by definition, those principles that accurately are associated with a given result or outcome.

___

[23] John Greenleaf Whittier (1807-1892) American writer.; Thinkexist/quotes

Capacity vision is really just a way of telling your mind that there is a path to your goal clear of fear-producing obstacles. It allows you to keep a clear vision of your goal. It reminds you that there are time-proven, correct principles associated with natural laws. It helps you associate your actions and the result. It keeps the mind's shutters open and allows you to take actions that will produce positive results.

Learning to clearly visualize your goal and to associate the correct principles which will provide a clear path to your goal is a prerequisite to increasing personal integrity. Capacity vision affirmations repeated daily with emotion are essential to training the mind to clearly visualize. Through exercising our capacity vision, we can repetitively convince the mind of what we can become and that the path to our goal is safe.

To illustrate the power of visualizing a goal and making it happen, consider the case of Aron Ralston. Aron Ralston, 27, was trapped in a remote slot canyon in Utah for five days. He was solo canyoneering[24] on a Saturday afternoon in Blue John Canyon, adjacent to the Maze District of Canyonlands National Park in southeastern Utah, when an 800-pound boulder fell on him, pinning his right arm. Ralston, who had only planned for a one-day hike, was unable to move and was trapped. His backpack contained two burritos, less than a liter of water, a cheap imitation of a Leatherman brand multi-tool, a small first aid kit, a video camera, a digital camera and rock climbing gear. The backpack did not contain a jacket or extra clothing.

Within the first hour after becoming trapped Ralston had calculated his options and came up with four possible solutions. They are as follows:

---

[24] Canyoneering is where a climber uses rock-climbing skills, ropes, and gear to negotiate narrow slot canyons.

- Someone would happen along and rescue him.
- He would be able to chip away at the rock and free his hand.
- He would be able to rig up something with the ropes and the equipment he had to move the rock.
- If all else failed, he would need to sever the arm.[25]

Death was a fifth possibility that Ralston didn't even want to think about. After three days, he ran out of water. On the fifth day Ralston realized that his survival required drastic action and that no one was going to save him but himself, so he grimly amputated his arm below the elbow using his pocketknife. He then applied a tourniquet and administered first aid from a kit that he had in his backpack. Then, with one arm, he rigged anchors and fixed a rope to rappel about 75 feet to the floor of Blue John Canyon, where he then continued hiking downstream into Horseshoe Canyon. That was where he was spotted by a search helicopter from the Utah Department of Public Service, which was sent out to search for Ralston after coworkers in Aspen reported that he hadn't been seen for four days.

"He was in some kind of bandage holding his arm up against his chest, and he had it all wrapped up," rescuers reported.

Ralston was transported to Allen Memorial Hospital in Moab, Utah, where he was stabilized and was later airlifted to St. Mary's in Grand Junction for further treatment. Ralston was an avid outdoors man and in exceptional physical condition.

"I've never seen anyone who has the will to live and is as much of a warrior as Aron is, and I've been doing this for twenty-five years. He is a warrior . . . Period!" expressed Steve Swanke, supervisory park ranger at Canyonlands National Park.

Ralston, an experienced climber, had climbed forty-five of the fifty-nine 14,000-foot peaks in Colorado solo in the

---

[25] http://www.climb-utah.com/Roost/bluejohn2.html; used with permission of Shane Burrows.

wintertime, and this outing was a warm-up for an upcoming ascent of North America's highest mountain, 20,320-foot tall Mount McKinley (Denali), in Alaska. Searchers returned by helicopter that same afternoon to the canyon where Ralston was trapped to try and retrieve his arm. They spotted it under the huge boulder, which they estimated at between 800 and 1000 pounds, but were unable to move it. Ralston's strong powers of visualization had outweighed his fear of pain, embarrassment, and ridicule, and this is what ultimately saved his life. Ralston overcame the illusion that help was on the way and he was able to take action that none of us would ever want to take. Yet it is critical for us to learn to take   action.[26]

Without action nothing happens.

Affirmations of what the goal might be must be visualized, but visualizations are not enough. You must also visualize the path clear of obstacles. The only way to do this is to recognize the correct principles–the statements of cause and effect, the laws that lead to the result.

Sarah Hughes understood this principle at an early age. She knew she had the potential, understood the laws, resolved to follow the principles and could visualize the result. It is said that she told her parents at age six, "I can't wait to go to the Olympics and win the Gold medal!"

She won the bronze medal in the 2001 Winter Olympics, and the gold medal in Women's Figure Skating in the 2002

---

[26] In November, 2010, a movie entitled, "127 Hours," portraying Aron Ralston's ordeal was released starring James Franco, and directed by Danny Boyle.

Winter Olympics. Knowing the correct principles bolsters confidence in obtaining the desired result.

What Do We Really Want?

We are bombarded by seductive messages of consumerism every day. Buying new cars, becoming beautiful people, and taking expensive vacations are what we are constantly told will make us happier. Divorces and marital distress may make us look to materiality rather than relationships for our happiness. One reason that people turn to materialism is to overcome emotional distress or insecurity. The overwhelming evidence tells us that materiality and consumerism do not bring satisfaction or happiness to the individual.

In research spanning a decade, Dr. Richard Ryan and Dr. Tim Kasser attempted to find a relationship between the American dream and happiness. Ryan and Kasser reported that their studies provided a look at the dark side of the American dream, noting that the culture in some ways seemed to be built on principles that are detrimental to mental health.

"Americans are encouraged to try to strike it rich, but the more we seek satisfactions in material goods, the less we find them there," Ryan stated. "The satisfaction has a short half-life; it's very fleeting. The more emphasis people put on worldly gains, the less happy they appear to be. It's the people who invest in intrinsic, personal satisfactions who are the contented ones."[27]

To illustrate the point, reflect on lottery winners in the United States. Studies of lottery winners have led psychologists to some startling conclusions:

- Immediately after winning, lottery winners are happier. This happiness lasts for about eight weeks.

---

[27] Kasser, T., and Ryan, R. M. (1993) "A Dark Side of the American Dream: Correlates of Financial Success as a Central Life Aspiration." Journal of Personality and Social Psychology, 65, p. 410-422.

- After eight weeks, lottery winners' happiness levels go back to where they were before winning.

- Winners in an Illinois study even rated simple pleasures like watching television, eating breakfast, or hearing a joke as less pleasurable than before winning.

Other researchers in the United States have attempted to find links between happiness and possessions. Findings show only very small correlations of around 10% or less between ownership of physical goods and happiness. Even these correlations are primarily due to differences between the very poor and the non-poor. Among the non-poor, the correlations between possessions and happiness become negligible. Clearly, having more money or possessions does not lead to happiness.

There is one grand key to achieving happiness in our lives. The key is charity.

Charity will drive away our irrational fears, allowing us to take action in accordance with correct principles, and thus develop both capacity and security. Charity is the act of putting the emotional and physical needs of other people before our own comforts. Phrased another way, we lack charity when we put our own comforts above the emotional and physical needs of others. When we consciously choose charity, our rationalizations and our fears of failure, ridicule, etc., fade away. Then we can clearly see and take the action that leads to positive results in our lives and in the lives of others. Self-focus invites inaction. Focusing on others invites action. It is a truism that the only way to find happiness is through making others happy.

The four fundamental results of charity are:

- **Love**

There is no greater need in our lives than the need to love and be loved. We need certain significant people in our lives to accept us and affirm us for who we are with all of our successes and failures, with all our good points and bad, with all of our ordinary ways and all our weaknesses or differences. We all need to feel loved just the way we are.

- **Respect**

We all seek affirmation from those around us (loved ones, colleagues, and acquaintances). The need to feel respected is critical to boosting our self-image and raising our confidence to accomplish our goals.

- **Acceptance**

We can't live as islands in our lives. We are all part of groups. Each of us is a member of a family, a community, a work group, and so forth. Feeling accepted by the group is also critical to self-esteem and high levels of performance.

- **Trust**

Being trusted emerges from being trustworthy. Feeling trusted affirms to us that we are trustworthy, that we can make and keep commitments. Trust boosts our ability to say "I can do it!"

These four fundamental results act as a spin cycle to propel us toward increased integrity and the resultant increase in both capacity and security. Let's take a closer look at each of these four categories.

Love

At a fundamental level, some people never feel loved. This is tragic in many ways. Frankly, some people are born into families with parents who are not capable of love. They have no capacity to love, and they have not learned to love even their own selves. How could they then show love to their children? This can be the most tragic circumstance of life.

Love is life's most important correct principle.

You cannot love without integrity. Love without integrity is false. It is pretended. It is not real and it will not bring the benefits to the lover or the loved. Yet love, unfeigned or real (with integrity) can be the most impacting and beautiful experience of life. It far transcends wealth, health, beauty, or power. Only those who are assured of their own integrity can give it. Only those assured of their own integrity can feel it.

So how do we become assured of our own integrity? How can we become sufficiently selfless to truly love others? How can we become so outwardly-oriented that we can put the needs of others ahead of our own needs? You cannot fake an outward focus. Many politicians try this, but usually the public can see through their facades. The truth will inevitably surface and the politicians' lusts, or self-interests, become blazingly apparent. There is an even more important reason why we cannot fake it. We will know that we are faking an outward focus. We know our own hearts perfectly, whether we admit it or not.

It is interesting that nearly every religion and many great philosophers have had the same recipe for successful relations with others.

- Christian Golden Rule: Do unto others as you would have them do unto you. (Luke 6:29-38); Thou shalt love thy neighbor as thyself. (Luke 10:27)

- Confucius: What you do not want done to yourself, do not do to others.

- Plato: May I do to others as I would that they should do unto me.

- Aristotle: We should behave to our friends as we wish our friends to behave to us.

- Judaism: What you hate, do not do to anyone.

- Islam: No one of you is a believer until he loves for his brother what he loves for himself.

- Buddhism: Hurt not others with that which pains thyself.

- Hinduism: Do nothing to thy neighbor which thou wouldst not have him do to thee.

- Sikhism: Treat others as you would be treated yourself.

If it is impossible to even fake this virtue, how can we develop it? We have known people who have been raised in homes with parents incapable of love and yet they have felt loved. Could it be that there is a way to feel loved in an environment where love is not present? It has to follow that there is love present in the environment, but it is a love of self, not to be confused with the oxymoron, selfish love. Love is a choice, which can only be made by people of integrity. Only people who respect themselves, who accept themselves, and who trust themselves are capable of creating an environment of love.

<u>Respect</u>

You cannot love yourself if you do not respect yourself. Respect is defined as deferential regard. To have self-respect is to have confidence in one's own abilities and decisions. People who are self-assured and have self-respect often enjoy the respect of others. Self-respect comes from our ability to accept ourselves. Just as there are acceptance criteria for getting into social groups or clubs, there are certain criteria that we set for our own self-acceptance. We are the only ones who really know whether or not we have met the requirements for self-acceptance. We cannot be fooled. When we consistently meet these criteria, we gain the ability to accept ourselves. The criteria we set for ourselves are based entirely on what we know we should be and do. If we know that we should be doing something other than what we are doing, we lack self-respect. We set our own standard. While there are a variety of standards that society might expect of us, socially-dictated standards do not matter nearly as much as personal standards in determining the level of self-respect we develop.

Integrity creates an environment of respect

A poem illustrates the relationship between integrity and respect for self. It is called "The Guy in the Glass," and was written by Dale Wimbrow (1895-1954).[28]

The Guy in The Glass

When you get what you want in your struggle for pelf,
And the world makes you King for a day,
Then go to the mirror and look at yourself,
And see what that guy has to say.

For it isn't your Father, or Mother, or Wife,
Who judgement upon you must pass.
The feller whose verdict counts most in your life
Is the guy staring back from the glass.

He's the feller to please, never mind all the rest,
For he's with you clear up to the end,
And you've passed your most dangerous, difficult test
If the guy in the glass is your friend.

---

[28] Used with permission by the children of Dale Wimbrow, Peter Dale Wimbrow Jr. and Sallydale Wimbrow.

You may be like Jack Horner and "chisel" a plum,
And think you're a wonderful guy,
But the man in the glass says you're only a bum
If you can't look him straight in the eye.

You can fool the whole world down the pathway of years,
And get pats on the back as you pass,
But your final reward will be heartaches and tears
If you've cheated the guy in the glass

The poem illustrates that we have to live with ourselves first and foremost and only we know ourselves best. We cannot fool ourselves.

A story from long ago illustrates the value of respect for others, that can only be demonstrated when one has self-respect.[29]

On a certain memorable occasion, in days gone by, a number of Greeks assembled at an Athenian theatre to see the acting of a "star" of primitive times. The Spartan ambassador and his countrymen occupied a part of the house opposite that allotted to the Athenian aristocracy. When the actor had gotten about half through, and during an intermission in the play, it happened that an old man, a citizen of Athens, came in, whose head was white with the snows of age. The young Athenian aristocrats resolved to have a joke at his expense, and therefore, pretending to make place for him, beckoned that he should come amongst them and take a seat. He did so,

---

[29] George Victor Le Vaux in <u>The Journal of Education for Ontario,</u> Volumes 23-34; Adolphus Egerton Ryerson, John George Hodgins, Adam Crooks. Ontario Department of Education; November 1872.

but when about to sit down, the "wags" closed in from either side and reoccupied the vacant space. They then laughed at the chagrin of the old man.

The gallant young Spartans, having observed this rude and insolent "performance," every man of them rose instantaneously, and remained standing whilst one of their number went over to the old gentleman and begged permission to conduct him to a seat. The old man complied, and leaning on the arm of the noble youth, crossed to the other side of the house, where he was requested to take the most honorable seat. Having done so, the whole band of Spartans quietly resumed their seats.

The people in the galleries, having observed this noble conduct, cheered and re-cheered the gallant Sacaddemonians, and the rude Athenians, now blushing at their own conduct, held down their heads with shame. Both parties received their reward—remorse the lot of the one, and an approving conscience the glory of the other. When the cheers had died away, the worthy sage arose, and after thanking the kind foreigners for their kind attention and example, expressed his regret that his fellow citizens, knowing what was right, did what was wrong; but was glad to find the Spartans practiced what the Athenians knew.

Respect is much more than mere self-acceptance. Respect for others is a universally correct principle which people of integrity recognize and implement in their actions.

<u>Acceptance</u>

Acceptance is the driving force behind much of the behavior exhibited in society. We follow rules of etiquette, fashion, speech, etc., because we desire to be accepted. Social mores are observations of what we find acceptable as a society. Deviance drives rejection in one group, but possible acceptance amongst the deviants. We all want to be accepted—it is just a matter of what group we want to join. This appears to be a basic human need.

Advertisers focus on our yearning for acceptance more than any other human appetite. 'If we drive a certain car, we will be accepted. If we look a certain way, we will be accepted. If we use a particular make-up product, we will be accepted. If we wear a certain brand of clothing, we will be accepted.'

As an example of the need to feel accepted, research into gang behavior has shown that young people join gangs to feel accepted. In a sense, the gang becomes a mechanism for surviving social deprivation and trauma. Gangs come into existence and flourish because the needs of the young people in a neighborhood or culture or family are not being met. The gang, in essence, fills the void.

Just as with love, there are examples of people who have been rejected by their friends, but still feel accepted. Why? Because they know they have done all that they should do and they trust themselves to do all that they need to do. They can accept themselves because of their integrity.

<u>Trust</u>

You cannot respect, love, or accept yourself if you do not trust yourself. You cannot trust another person if he or she is constantly making and breaking commitments to you. You cannot trust yourself if you fail to make and keep commitments to yourself.

**You have integrity,
if you make and keep
commitments to yourself.**

You will gain great respect for yourself as you exercise the moral muscle of making and keeping commitments to yourself. Trust is the foundation upon which all societies are based. Even a secret combination of thieves is based on a foundation of trust within their own ranks. Social interaction is impossible without trust.

Integrity is directly associated with the development of capacity.   Taking daily action in the direction of our goals—by making and keeping commitments based on correct principles— will give you more ability than not acting or acting upon incorrect principles. In order to do this you must know what you want. You must know specifically and clearly what you want. You cannot develop integrity without making decisions about what you want. Once you are clear regarding what it is that you want, you need to understand the laws upon which your goals are predicated. Then you must decide how you are going to specifically act in accordance with those laws. It is the process of self management. You can't start until you know where you are going.

A trustworthy character begins with the little things. So-called big moral decisions, such as what to do with an apparent opportunity to take large sums of money from a company or from others are not made in a vacuum. The decision to be trustworthy must start with little, seemingly unimportant decisions.

A friend of mine, Steve Albrecht, accompanied two convicted felons who had each embezzled millions of dollars, and spent a day lecturing to college students One of the embezzlers stated that it was the *SUDs,* (seemingly unimportant decisions) that he had made that led him to his dishonest actions. He started out an honest and trustworthy businessman, but over time he started rationalizing the little things that were slightly dishonest, but seemed trivial at the time. These small moral compromises were repeated over and over until he became desensitized. He seared his conscience until it no longer knew right from wrong. He could not even trust himself.

A Hollywood executive once related about the person he admired most. This seasoned executive disclosed that he admired Donny Osmond at the top of his list. When asked why, he stated that "it was because of Donny's high level of integrity." Late one night in the Osmond family studio, he observed the following incident:

> Donny was thirsty after a long rehearsal and they were out of drinks. There was a vending machine in the facility. Donny hit the vending machine just right, and to his surprise, a soda can came out. He drank the soda and left, but shortly afterward he returned to the studio (which was owned by his own family) and placed money in

the machine to pay for the soda. This act of integrity so impressed the executive, that he always felt comfortable in any dealings with Donny because of his integrity as demonstrated that night.

So what is it that you really want? Will the goods that advertisers pedal bring you satisfaction? Do you think that the beauty, wealth, fame, and sex they falsely promote will bring you happiness?

CHAPTER 8

WHAT IS CAPACITY?

Capacity is the ability
to accomplish worthwhile goals.

Capacity is difficult to measure by looking at outward evidences of success—a person with great capacity may not appear to seek worldly success. Yet, relevant outward measures are the level of respect, trust, and love that flows to a person, and the level of trust, respect, and love that person has for himself or herself.

Interestingly, each of us has equal or potential capacity to strive for and accomplish whatever goals we choose! This point is very critical to understand. Some might believe that one person has more capacity to accomplish than does another, because that first person seems to achieve better results. This simply is not true. What is true is that the achiever has learned how to develop and use more of their capacity to accomplish goals.

Consider the case of twins on the same little league baseball team. Both twins were blessed with tremendous athletic ability. Both had the talent to be the best players on their team. However, one twin had much more ambition to practice than the other one. When they first started playing little league baseball, it was difficult to know which of the two would perform best. However, by the time they graduated from little league baseball at age 12, there was a considerable difference in their talent levels. The young man who persistently practiced on a consistent, regular basis became the star pitcher and hitter in the entire league, while his twin was relegated to being a substitute player.

Why is it important to distinguish that our capacity isn't limited, but that our behaviors and habits limit our ability to use our capacity? It is one thing to believe that a certain individual is simply more capable, better educated, smarter, and has more time. Using that logic, we can find excuses to ignore the real cause of the differences (capacity). It is quite another to believe that you have the capacity to achieve your worthwhile goals, and by simply learning how and training yourself to do it, you can fundamentally change your life and your attainment. If you believe this, you can never say to yourself, "I can't do it; I'm never going to make it."

When you think in a positive manner, you choose to step on the treadmill of self-improvement and accomplishment.

Two Ways to Reach Your Goals

There are basically two ways to improve your performance to attain your goals:

First, you can develop more capacity to perform. The process is not difficult, but it requires discipline and commitment on your part. It is largely associated with developing greater integrity.

The second way is to consciously choose better how to manage your capacity. A good example is the management of your time. Rather than watch television, you could choose to spend your time engaged in accomplishing your more worthwhile goals.

The interesting thing about these two methods is that they are linked. Think about it. Why would someone with the potential to accomplish his or her goals waste time day after day not doing it? The answer is simple. They don't realize or haven't learned they can! They fear failure. They haven't really developed the capacity to accomplish their goals. They are most likely allowing self-doubt to stand in their way, and rather than try–they give up.

The Basis of Forming Capacity

Study and ponder the diagram on the next page for a few minutes and let the words and picture soak in. This picture is the key to understanding how you can develop personal capacity. You will see that there are two circles, one focused on personal acceptance, the other on outward acceptance. Note that the circle for personal acceptance is inside the circle for outward acceptance. Notice that the labels are numbered telling you that there is order and sequence to the process of developing capacity.

The Capacity Cycle

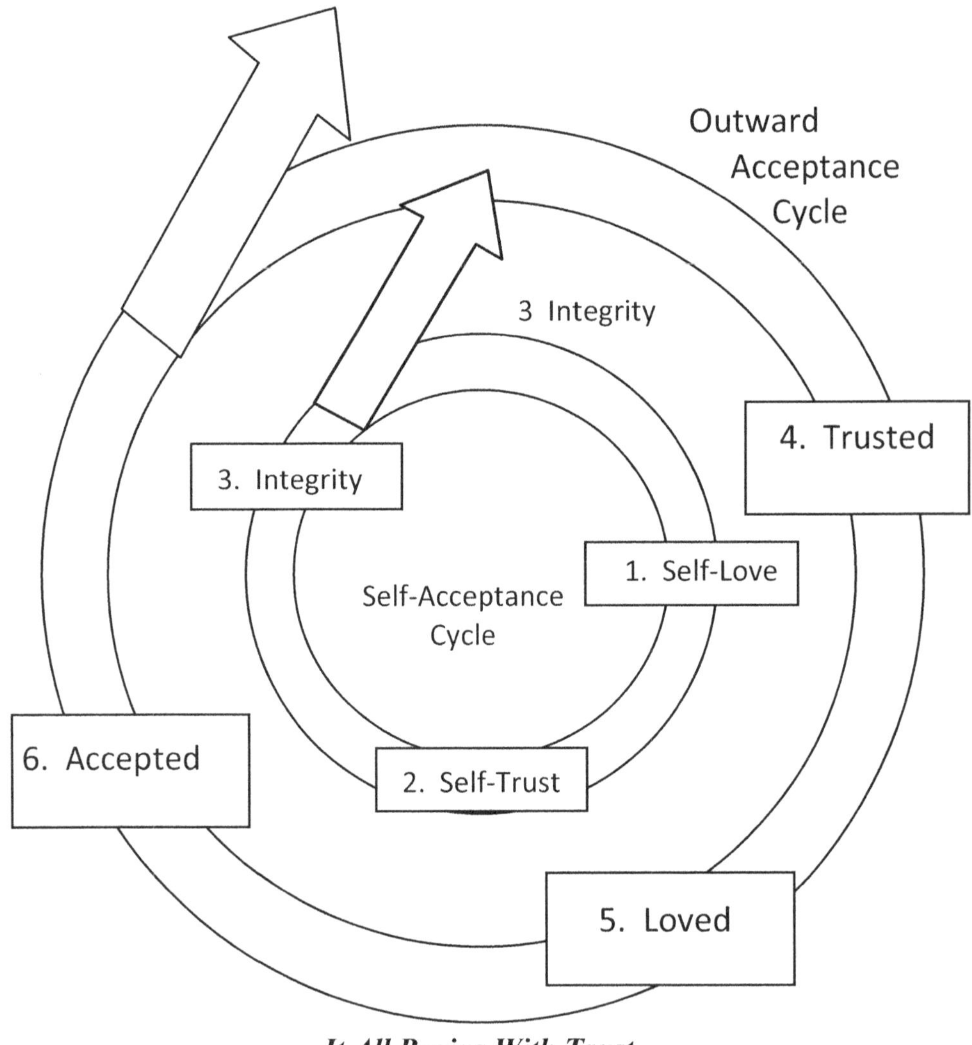

It All Begins With Trust

Diagram adapted from drawing by The Boston Consulting Group

CHAPTER 9

SELF-TRUST
THE BASIS OF INTEGRITY

**Self-trust is
the basis of integrity.**

Your self-image and self-respect is based on your perfect self-knowledge No one else in this world knows you as well as you do. Can you always be trusted? When you make a commitment to yourself or to someone else, do you always keep it? When you know what you should be doing, do you always do it? Are you always truthful with yourself?

If you are truthful with yourself—like most people, you will see areas for improvement. If you answered yes to all of the foregoing questions, there is no need for you to read further—you are a person of perfect integrity and unlimited capacity.

Is there anyone who does not want to improve their personal capacity? With increased capacity, we can have additional ability to serve our families, our communities, our respective nations, our youth, our churches, and our businesses. With increased capacity, we are able to make a difference and leave a lasting legacy. With increased capacity, we can experience greater freedom and feel better about ourselves.

It stands to reason, then, to develop greater integrity, the first step in the process is to develop greater self-trust. The way to develop greater self-trust is to prove yourself to be trustworthy. This can be accomplished by a series of exercises designed to increase our self-experience of trustworthiness.

My parents always made their bed together every morning when they got up. Mother stated that it was important to do because it built self-esteem. They continued this ritual throughout their lives. This is a simple exercise (or example), but it demonstrates self- discipline. It took many years for me to make the connection and finally understand the wisdom my mother was trying to teach. Resolving to make your bed every morning, without fail, and always doing what you resolve is a daily exercise that will help you develop a sense of self-trust.

As you build up more and more experiences of self-trust, you will experience growing self-respect. As your self-respect grows, you will be less inhibited by your fears, which are created by false associations. You will then have a greater capability to see and implement correct principles into your life. As you do this, your capacity or power will increase. This will happen because you will now be acting on truths—on things as they really are. In a world where people think the world is flat, you will know that it is round.

A parent will realize the value in creating opportunities for his children to have successes. Just like the making the bed example in the previous paragraph, having children experience small successes will help build their self esteem and respect. This will help children have the confidence to know they can accomplish tasks. A wise parent looks for as many opportunities for their children to experience success in making and keeping commitments as possible. Whether these successes occur in sports, school, music, or other facets of life–it isn't the primary activity that is important but rather the feeling of accomplishment, self-trust and self-respect that comes from taking action and getting results.

Again, integrity begins with self-trust. If you do not trust yourself to follow through and keep your commitments, you will be increasingly reluctant to make commitments. For obvious reasons (all men have conscience), it becomes difficult for us to live with ourselves if we break our commitments. Whenever we do, we immediately engage in the rationalization process and our views of reality become distorted. That is why it is important to begin by making small commitments to yourself that you can easily keep, such as making your bed every day. In the big scheme of things, this does not seem like a life-critical commitment to make. However, it is precisely for that very reason that it is a good commitment to make in order to begin the process of developing self-trust.

By the time we are making life-critical commitments, we'd better be sure our self-trust muscle is very strong. It is the equivalent of going to the gym everyday to strengthen our physical muscles. Our exertions at the gym produce results–the strengthening of our physical muscles. Thus conditioned, our physical muscles have a greater capacity to do real work. So it is with our self-trust muscle. We can strengthen both through a process of small commitments that we always keep.

A good example of the value of small commitments is in exercising. A daily exercise routine can not only help us become physically stronger, but can help us improve psychologically as well. The psychological benefits of exercise are often overlooked. Today's society greatly focuses on the physical benefits of exercise, such as weight loss, toned muscles, and endurance. Although these are remarkable benefits, the psychological benefits can be just as, if not more, significant than the physical benefits. Just making and keeping a commitment builds self-respect and self-trust.

What are the psychological benefits of exercise? There are many psychological benefits of physical activity. The most common are:

- Decreased Daily and Chronic Stress
  Exercise is one of the best ways to decrease stress by the release of endorphins and by creating an outlet from daily tension and anxiety.

- Improved Self-Confidence and Body Image
  By exercising regularly, most people will begin to see positive physical change. When individuals start seeing these results, they tend to be proud of their success and feel good about who they are.

- Enhanced Moods
  Those who consistently exercise have a more positive outlook and are happier overall in comparison to the inactive population.

- Alleviate Depression
  Studies show that regular exercise can greatly reduce and in some cases prevent the symptoms of depression.

- Increased Mental Alertness
  A regular exercise routine will enhance mental alertness and can improve overall mental health.

- Increased Self-Discipline
  A regular exercise routine will help you develop self-discipline in other areas of value.

Have you ever noticed how people who have resolved to practice an hour a day and actually do it have greater capacity to play a musical instrument than those who do not make the same type of resolve? They also seem to have more capacity than those who make the resolve and don't practice. In fact, the latter often drop out of the program and have excuses for why they no longer play an instrument. There are many rationalizations but they fall into certain categories. They are:

- Lack of Talent

- Lack of Desire

- Lack of Agency

- Lack of Time

The truth is, if they made and kept the resolution, they would somehow find the talent, desire, agency, and time.

Life itself consists of what we resolve to do and what we actually do. Capacity is developed as we become stronger and stronger in our ability to make and keep resolutions. This process is obviously two-fold and can begin at a very early age. There must be:

(1) resolve, and (2) action

In order for there to be resolve, we must first visualize the result or goal we desire to obtain. A process that works must be identified. We must know what actions will get us to the vision we have resolved to attain. We must commit to do the actions regardless of obstacles in our way. Then we can enjoy the fruits of achieving our resolve. We begin to learn this process of life early, even before we can walk.

When we become efficient at taking daily action in the direction of our goals, we will trust ourselves. It becomes clear that we have the power to take the actions we commit to take, and that will carry over into the commitments we make to others. Soon we will have a reputation for trustworthiness, and our bosses and associates will have confidence that if we are asked to take an action, it will be done. It is this self-trust that is the very foundation for developing integrity. Many people do not make commitments to take daily action, even to themselves. They do not trust themselves to carry through and complete the commitment. In this state of mind, integrity is impossible.

You develop integrity by making and keeping daily commitments. Hold yourself accountable. Consider getting a capacity coach–someone trained to help you visualize your goals, make daily commitments to take action, and hold you accountable.

On the following page, list some of the daily actions you feel you could or would like to commit to at this time:

CHAPTER 10
INTEGRITY LIMITATIONS

What interferes with taking action toward our goal

One of the most important things we can do in developing greater personal capacity is to understand what holds us back. It is an integral part of the process. There are multiple reasons why we do not take the actions that we know will result in the consequences we desire. Some of these are:

- Self deception through rationalization

- Rebellion and revenge

- Fear

- Lack of confidence or self-image

- Failure to make decisions

- False associations

First, we must be aware that we are being held back. Then we must figure out what is causing the problem and face those issues head-on. There is no short cut.

Rationalization

The human mind cannot stand incongruence. If our actions do not meet our standards, we will quickly either change our behavior or lower our standards. This is the process of rationalization.

Interestingly enough, false victories often hold us back. Sometimes, as we walk down the path of life, someone comes from nowhere and gives us a good job, we obtain a better house, a better-equipped or fancier car . . . and life seems pretty good. The basic problem with this is that the good we enjoy might make us miss the fact that it is the process which is more important than the result in building our own personal capacity. Is it possible that someone with a good job, a better house, and a luxurious car, could feel unloved, not respected, incapable, or not trusted? Of course, it is possible.

**We are not defined by what we possess,
but by what we process.**

We are what we are due to the processes we have experienced along our chosen path. Reflect on inherited wealth. One lawyer who has helped many individuals in the process of inheriting wealth stated, "There hasn't been a lot written about the dark side to acquiring inherited wealth and there really is a dark side."

Inherited wealth tends to nurture paranoia, not self-worth. It tends to wall wealthy heirs off from others, and make trusting relationships with spouses and friends incredibly difficult. Those with significant inherited wealth find that they don't automatically become happier because of their wealth. There is an old saying, "Riches to rags in three generations." When people obtain the possession without the procession, the possession is hard to enjoy and keep. It is a hollow victory because it is the process that refines and qualifies. This is not to say that those who inherit wealth cannot recognize the laws, take action, build self-trust and become people of great integrity, but it is not automatic.

Rebellion and Revenge

Rebellion is defined as resistance to or defiance of any authority, control, or tradition. Rebellion is good when we are resisting or defying tyranny or evil. But when we rebel against true and correct principles, we fail to take action in accordance with truth and cut off our capacity. Many a child rebels against the correct teachings of their parents only to later find themselves on the road their parents warned them about, often a one way street. But in everyday life we should challenge ourselves by asking, "What great principles and teachings am I rebelling against and what is the cost?"

Revenge is a method of deflecting our attention away from ourselves and onto another person whom we feel has harmed us in some way. It is the opposite of the divine principle of forgiveness, and is rarely or fleetingly satisfying. Once revenge is extracted, it leaves us empty. Revenge also becomes a mental, emotional and physical compulsion that overwhelms our time and space.

Fear

Fear of Pain

Have you ever been paralyzed by fear? It is characterized by the inability to take action due to an overriding and usually false association between the action and pain. Fear is natural. We can develop our integrity muscle by overcoming fear. It is similar to the resistance principle that we use in the gym when developing muscles. If we do what we know we should do, in spite of the resistance we feel, our ability to take action will increase.

Fear is one of the greatest capacity limitations that exist. Fear operates the shutter in our minds that keeps us from visualizing the possibilities or seeing our true self-images. There is very little that we should fear. Studies have shown that people who have little fear have longevity in line with the general population. Some people have a fear of flying. Statistically, they have no better chance of living longer than people who do fly. Yet it is not necessarily the big things, like flying, that seem to challenge us most.   Often it is the little fears that hold us back, such as fear of success, fear of failure, fear of public speaking, fear of emotional attachment, etc. Studies have shown that many people do not report wrong-doing in companies because of fear. Usually they fear either retribution or apathy from their managers. One study found that 60% of corporate frauds go unreported.

A few years ago, a machine foreman at a major U.S. manufacturing company stood up at an assertiveness training session, and told the class that the company was ripping off the government. He confided in approximately 30 colleagues, stating that the time cards going into the supervisor's offices were not the same ones coming out. Within a few minutes several other foremen stood up to confirm his story. Even after his outburst in the assertiveness class, the foreman's superiors still pressured him to coax his subordinates to cheat on their time cards. He was told that if his subordinates would not alter their own time cards, he was to do so. When he refused, his supervisors altered the cards for him.

According to this foreman, the process was hardly subtle. "With black or blue felt-tipped pens, the supervisors altered the billing vouchers. Usually they scrawled the number of a project safely within cost constraints over the number of a job that was already running over budget."

Foremen who refused to falsify vouchers had their vouchers sent to the unit manager, who would then complete the blank vouchers himself. When the unit manager died, his successor continued the falsification of time cards and billing vouchers. At one time, this man told the foreman the company was like a great big pie, and that everyone who participated (in cheating) got a piece; those who did not participate did not get a slice.

Falsifying at this plant had become a way of life. One foreman confessed to personally altering 50-60% of his subordinates' time cards during an eight-month period. Once, when the foreman told his superior that he could go to jail for altering cards, the reply was that he was only carrying out orders and that there was not any chance of getting caught.

Finally, the foreman decided he needed to alert someone who could do something about the problem. One weekend he slipped into a secretary's office and photocopied about 150 altered time cards and billing vouchers. He wrote an eight-page letter explaining what had been going on. The next week, he delivered the letter and the photocopies to the senior vice-president in charge of the plant.

The same day, the whistle-blower was dismissed. A subsequent investigation by the FBI and the Defense Contract Audit Agency revealed that $7.2 million of idle time had been falsely billed to the U.S. government. They also discovered that 27% of the time-sheet vouchers in the shop where he worked had been falsified during the prior three years.

In this case, the foreman's tips were the sole reason fraud was detected. Certainly his supervisors did not make it easy for him to come forward. This fraud highlights many of the mistakes that companies make regarding informants. Even though the foreman knew that fraud was occurring, the firm's punishment and intimidation of whistle-blowers and not making it easy to come forward allowed the dishonesty to be concealed for a long time. It created an environment of fear.

The foreman demonstrated great integrity in difficult circumstances.

What kinds of Pain do we Fear?

Physical Pain

A person had a fear of dentists from the time he was young. He was convinced his physical senses were heightened beyond most others, and going to the dentist became a painful experience. Even as a man, he was reticent to try a new dentist, and was saddened when his dentist retired. Soon afterward, this man was required to live in another country where physicians and dentists were in short supply and even then, he was reluctant to use one. After suffering from a severe toothache for several weeks, he finally acquiesced to try a dentist who had been recommended by a friend. It turned out he thought the dentist was as good as his former retired dentist back home! His fears were totally unfounded.

Emotional Pain

Why do we withdraw? What do we withdraw from? Sometimes we have a hard time coping with the circumstances that we are dealt. Why? Often our fear becomes so great that we stop trying. We feel this fear at an emotional level. Even though we know intellectually that we must stay on track to achieve the desired result, we stop taking action in the direction of our goal. It might be a fear that we will never be loved for who we are. It might be a fear that we will not accomplish our goal and that failure would bring humiliation. Whatever the fear is, we experience it at an emotional level. Fear is an emotion, not a real fact.

Intellectual Pain

This fear is one of the most frustrating. Many people fail to develop their intellect because of false beliefs. One false belief that can be passed from generation to generation is the belief that a family is "blue collar" or "just farmers," or simply " not very smart." These people often do not take the development of their intellect seriously, because they already believe they are less equipped to succeed. The interesting thing is it has been demonstrated that most people are smart enough, yet only the ones who are persistent and stick to the task eventually achieve intellectual success. While attending college, one of my friends and mentors was a professor named Cleon Skousen. Professor Skousen would often make the remark that the only difference between a PhD degree and anyone else was persistence.

It's not necessary to end up with a PhD, but you can continually develop your intellect through the study and application of every worthwhile field of endeavor. The true aim of education is the development of character. Life is measured by the sum of our actions. Intellectual development is the discovery of laws, the recognition of how to apply those laws, and the character to do so.

So why the pain? Why choose to feel that we are not smart enough? Why not get involved in life-long learning?

Spiritual Pain

Why are so many people so closed off to exploring their spiritual natures? We are living in the age of enlightenment. There is no denying that information we are exposed to via computers, iPads, and smart phones provide us with the opportunity to explore more than at any other time in history. Many family traditions, however, limit the exploration of other religions and belief systems. Religion addresses the spiritual development of our natures. If we fail to think of ourselves as both physical beings and spiritual beings, it can be possible to neglect the part of our nature that opens a wider view and draws us closer to God, truth, and each other.

I have always appreciated my wife's view of spiritual development. She wants to know everything that is out there. If there is anything that can bring her and her family more joy, more safety, more happiness, or closer to God–to add to the knowledge she has discovered so far, she wants to know about it. So do I.

Be believing! You cannot function without belief. You cannot have faith without first having belief. You cannot act without faith, or achieve results without acting.

"You can be anything you want to be, if only you believe with sufficient conviction and act in accordance with your faith; for whatever the mind can conceive and believe, the mind can achieve." [30]

The opposite is also true. If the mind cannot conceive and believe, it cannot achieve. Why? Because there is no capacity! We all begin this life having the simple faith of a child in learning simple things. As young babies, we were dependent upon the care of our parents and others around us to help us develop and learn. Many of us remember our fathers throwing us up in the air. With a little gasp and losing our breath, we knew their strong arms would catch us on the way down. Most of us probably don't remember the process of learning to walk, yet, with try after try, and fall after fall, each of us knew we could eventually stay up and walk. We knew many things because our parents and teachers told us, and we exhibited a simple child-like faith.

As we progress, we learn that the term faith actually relates to a belief in something unseen, yet true. Transforming simple child-like faith into a mature and sturdy faith doesn't just happen! It takes study, commitment, questioning, praying, trials and acceptance, and continuous effort. Our exercise of faith in true principles builds character; fortified character expands our capacity to exercise more faith.

Character strength is not developed in moments of great challenge or temptation. That is when character is demonstrated. Strong moral character results from consistent correct choices in the little trials of life. Such choices are made with trust in things that are believed, and when acted upon, are confirmed.

Faith is acting on your beliefs, but it is so much more. Faith is the underlying principle of all action. You cannot move your finger without demonstrating faith. Belief can be declared in words, but faith must be demonstrated by taking action. It is impossible to have faith in any principle, law, or person

---

[30] Napoleon Hill (1883-1970) American author; one of earliest producers of personal success literature.

without acting in accordance with the teachings of that principle, law, or person.

Fear of Failure

Many people quit before they ever begin. Nothing ventured and nothing gained. We falsely believe that if we do not take action, there will be no consequence.

So why do people fail to take the actions they know they need to take in order to accomplish a result? Sometimes the result is so emotionally important to achieve that we just cannot bear the risk that we might fall short of the result. We therefore take either half-hearted action, or no action at all. As mentioned earlier, in his book, *Outliers: Story of Success* (2008) Malcolm Gladwell talks about the necessity of putting in 10,000 hours of practical experience before one can become an expert at almost anything. Many people want to become a professional athlete or an accomplished musician, but those that do so put in the additional hours of practice and performance to make it happen. Those who fall short, usually put in 2000 hours, or 4000 hours, or maybe even 6000 hours and are able to perform, but never get to the level that people achieve who put in the full measure. There are many rationalizations that relate to intelligence, natural talent, etc., but the truth usually lies in the matter of how much time is invested in order to accomplish the set goal.

Why are we so afraid to fail? The most likely result of failure is that we learn or discover something. We learn which actions do not work to achieve a result, we learn what kind of effort will fall short of achieving the desired result, and we learn valuable lessons that we can apply to our next attempts. Some noteworthy failures include Abraham Lincoln, already mentioned, who made several attempts to gain political office prior to being elected president of the United States. The Wright brothers made several attempts to fly prior to their success, and Thomas Edison failed to produce a light bulb over 3,000 times before ushering in the dawn of electric lights.

There are very few reasons to let fear of failure stop us from taking appropriate actions. If you fear you cannot outrun an angry grizzly bear, you probably have good reason to not put the matter to a test, yet it is a fact that failing to take appropriate action toward a worthy goal due to a fear of failure is usually not rational.

Lack of Self-Confidence and Self-Image

We know what we fear. We know what we believe. However, we do not always know what we want. We do not always know why we have our fears that prevent us from taking action. We do not always understand how we learn, or what motivates us to take action. Much of what we think and believe has been handed down to us in the culture we were raised in.

Malcolm Gladwell, in *Outliers*, speaks about the culture of honor that developed in Kentucky during the feuding years most notably represented by the "Hatfields and the McCoys." It was demonstrated that they were acting based on long handed-down attitudes and cultural beliefs of their ancestors. They did not even realize why they were fighting to the death. Sometimes in life we need coaches and mentors who can help us see why we are behaving the way we are, and what steps we could take to get a different result. Everyone needs a coach. How could you benefit from having a personal coach?

Self-confidence is developed through knowing what actions to take to achieve a result, and consistently following through with actions. When you live in accordance with the laws, your confidence waxes strong. When you know what to do and actually do it, self-confidence grows, since you know you can achieve whatever it is you want by discovering and living by correct principles. Confidence is defined as belief in one's self and one's powers or abilities. Certainly you would believe in yourself if you knew how to always get consistent results by applying correct principles.

Self-image is the idea or mental conception that one has of one's self. It is the sum of your self-confidence and your beliefs. Self-image cannot improve by others telling us positive things, but improves by our actions. If we hold ourselves in low self-esteem, it is a reflection of our unwillingness to act in accordance with correct principles. Self-image is molded by our experiences with ourselves, and is a reflection of our integrity. We develop a low self-image by not acting in accordance with what we know we should be doing,especially if there are fears. False beliefs keep us from taking actions. A low self-image can be raised by a coach or a mentor who helps us realize why we are not acting as we know we should, and helps us know what motivates us to proper action. A coach holds you accountable.

A negative cycle produces negative results which we use to beat up our self-image. If you feel like you have a low self-image, you may want to consider a coach.

Failure to Make Decisions

Once upon a time there were five frogs sitting on a log. They were croaking and carrying on and enjoying each other's company on a bright sunny day. Three of the frogs decided to jump off the log. How many frogs were left on the log? The answer to the riddle is 5. The point being that merely deciding is not enough, you must also take the decided action. The decision always precedes the action. You cannot do anything that you do not first decide to do.

Many people have a hard time doing what they decide to do, but a far greater number never decide to do. Many of us want to do or to be something, but for various reasons we never decide to "go for it". We fail to realize that our decisions determine our destiny.

This failure to decide has far-reaching consequences. It is, of course a decision itself. You must decide to not decide. Have you ever been a part of an organization where the leader of the organization decided to not make a decision?

One organization in which the personal computer was first developed had their CEO resign. The parent company then had two men appointed to be "co-presidents." These men made a decision to not make any big decisions for the first year and half of their tenure. This decision, to not make decisions, allowed the technology world to pass them by, and they lost the business they had established. This devastating consequence ensued merely from not making major decisions. It impacted nearly 1000 good employees, their families, and the parent company and its shareholders.

We also fail to decide in our own personal decisions even when we full well know that we should be making a decision. What should I major in at college? Should we get married? Should I set aside time to study? Should we buy this house? Should I lose weight? Should we take a trip? Should I change jobs? The list goes on and on. There are many reasons why we put aside making decisions. Perhaps we think a better alternative will come along. Sometimes we think that we need to study the matter more to be sure we anticipate all of the potential consequences. Often we just fear failure or are influenced by some of the other action limiters discussed in this chapter.

It is important to develop the talent of making quick decisions. The decisions we make shape the actions we take and those actions have defined consequences. Therefore the quality of our decisions shape the result we get in life. Those who decide not to decide are making a decision to allow the operation of natural laws and the actions of others to determine their outcomes. People who are good at making decisions and taking actions in accordance with laws determine their own outcomes.

These people also get quick feedback if they happen to make a wrong decision. If they take the actions that they thought would lead to a consequence, and they are not getting the consequence—they can quickly make a new decision, adjust their actions, and get the consequence they were looking for. People who do not make decisions based on the knowledge of truth available to them fail to get this feedback simply because they are not taking actions.

<u>False Associations</u>

This is perhaps one of the main reasons that we do not take action in accordance with correct principles. As discussed in earlier chapters, our minds can believe a lie. We generally take actions in accordance with our beliefs and values. This is an extremely important concept to understand. Even when we repeatedly are not getting the results that we were promised, or that we expected, we can continue to act in accordance with a false association for years and years. Our minds are fully capable of believing something in spite of the clear evidence that surrounds us. As discussed earlier it is the principle upon which some marketing is based. Think how many people have died early from the false associations connected to tobacco or drugs.

While I am a believer in religion, I can see why so many are cynical, because historically many religions have used false associations to influence or control the actions and loyalties of their believers. False associations have stopped their believers from exploring actions and consequences and proving truth for themselves. Many people are willing to take extreme actions impacting negatively on the lives of thousands based on totally false associations prescribed by their religions. Religion should be a valuable tool in the discovery of truth and should encourage followers to discover truth from whatever source–whether it be dogma, books, history, science or testing principles in the laboratory of life.

How do we overcome false associations? We need to be open minded and find a mentor or coach, because we are blinded by false associations on our own. You are engaged in a practice that can help you remove false associations at this very moment by studying this book, pondering its meaning, and deciding to act on its principles. Coaching can come from books, family, counselors, life coaches and as a system of accountability. It is not about turning our lives over to coaches. The value of a coach is to help us see more of must be done–then we become the believers and the doers.

CHAPTER 11
CORRECT PRINCIPLES

Learn correct principles and act upon them to demonstrate true integrity.

"Everything is relative."

"There is no right and wrong."

"It really doesn't matter what you do or don't do."

"There are no moral absolutes."

"Do your own thing."

"Lying doesn't matter, because everybody does it."

"Go ahead! Take advantage of someone because you can."

"They would do it to you if they were in your position."

"There is no God or higher authority."

"There is no absolute truth."

"It is not what is real that is important, but what
you perceive as being real. Perception is everything."

"Contracts were made to be broken."

"Things change."

These are all popular idioms from our present day society–hangovers from the baby boom era and the early 1960's. Thoughts like these have led people into the low integrity, low capacity, and low result lifestyle. While promising ultimate freedom, they have delivered a form of bondage.

The truth is that truth is. While we may not have discovered all truth, we have discovered sufficient truth. The search for truth is, in effect, a search for natural laws. What are the laws that govern us? What are the exceptions to those laws, if any? How can we master the laws in such a way so when we take an action we can assure ourselves of getting a result? There are laws that govern our physical condition. Many of these laws are easily observable, yet others have taken years to discover. For many years we had no idea what caused people to get sick with infectious diseases.

A very interesting story is told about Dr. Ignaz Semmelweis, who was an obstetrician at the Vienna General hospital in Vienna, Austria. He could not figure out why the mothers in his ward experienced such a high degree of mortality compared to the mortality rate at some of the other hospitals in the surrounding area. Several things were attempted to alleviate the condition—better ventilation, rearrangement of the beds, closer attendance by the nursing staff, but nothing seemed to work. Dr. Semmelweis left Vienna General and visited another hospital for a period of time, and the mortality rate at the Vienna General hospital seemed to improve dramatically. He was stunned that the mortality rate possibly might be connected directly with him. As he reviewed the situation, he came up with a theory. Microscopic organisms were somehow attaching to him when he worked on cadavers in the adjacent ward, and subsequently infecting the women he was treating as he delivered their babies.

Until that time we did not understand the laws relating to germs and the spread of disease. For centuries these laws lay undiscovered. The solution that was implemented was simply the frequent washing of hands by the attending staff. Mortality rates decreased dramatically. A law, or statement of cause and effect, was discovered and appropriate action taken—the mere washing of hands.

We cannot purport in this book to elaborate all of the laws that have been discovered, but we can review some of the things that our preceding generations have discovered and passed on for our benefit. We will discuss a few of the laws that can have profound effects on our lives when we understand them and live them.

The analogy can be made of a farmer. If a farmer plants potatoes, barring other factors or actions, he will reap a crop of potatoes. It is at least clear that he will not reap a crop of corn if he plants potatoes. The rule is not intended to be a statement of absolute outcome, because there is no truth or law that operates in a complete vacuum. To a farmer, other influences or actions can influence whether or not he actually harvests a crop. These are things like the action of insects, weather, the market economy etc. However, it is surely a truth that he will not harvest a crop different than potatoes. That is an absolute truth. There are, indeed, absolute truths.

The Law of the Harvest applies to much more than farmers; the law applies to every aspect of our lives. We get out of life what we put into it. It applies to raising children and to leading employees. Generally speaking, what goes around comes around. How you treat your parents is a good indication of how your children will treat you. Just as with the potato farmer, the law does not operate in a vacuum and several factors can intervene, but the law applies to sociality much as it applies to farmers.

When I had just graduated from college and was living in a cramped apartment complex with thin walls, a single mother who lived next door was often heard screaming foul obscenities at her 4 year-old daughter. Later, I overheard the little girl yelling the very same obscenities at their kitten. She probably didn't even know of the import of the words she was repeating, but usage begets more usage.

What goes around comes around, as stated in the lyrics of a popular Harry Chapin song entitled "Cat's in the Cradle" by Sandy & Harry Chapin.[31] The lyrics tell the story of how every parent's actions set the example for our children and the importance of what we do rather than what we say. The lyrics tell of a child being born and growing up with a father too busy to be involved. The little boy idolized his father and always said, "I'm gonna be like you, dad."

The child is asking for time with his father, but the father is always procrastinating their time together, constantly promising he didn't know when, but they would get together soon and experience those father/son moments. Too late, the father realizes his son is all grown up and the tables are turned. Now the father wants to spend time with his son, but the son is much too busy. With sad realization, the father acknowledges his son had indeed grown up just like his father.

Understanding the Law of the Harvest is key to growth and development. It is the law of action and outcome. If we

---

[31] http://www.harrychapin.com/music/cats.html

take action we can expect consequence. The law is broader than the mere statement of we reap what we sow. In order to reap a harvest, we must not only plant, but weed, water, and shelter the growing crop from the actions of others or nature. As we seek to understand the interplay of actions that can affect the outcome, we learn to deal with the pests, keep others from trampling the tender plants, and understand what is required for the right amount of water and nutrients so the plants mature. Those who teach us that we are free to act without consequence are wrong and the root cause of evil. Those who idle their time away participating in pornography, raucous music, questionable partners, drugs and addiction, etc., cannot and will not escape the consequences. It may appear to be fun and games for a while, but there is always an inevitable price to be paid. There are consequences to every personal and political decision we make.

The great lie of the twentieth century was that you can make bad choices and escape the consequences. Millions have ruined their lives relying on this big lie. Yet, the lie is so big and appealing that millions continue in this course. Wouldn't it be nice if it were true? Actually the answer is a resounding **"NO!"** It would not be nice. It would be devastating because the law works both ways. It is morally neutral. Just as you cannot escape the consequences of bad choices, you cannot escape the consequences of good choices.

The valedictorian at a prominent high school gave the keynote address to her graduating class of 2003. The central theme of her speech was she had learned in high school that there is no such thing as good or bad, only different. This is not the truth, but has been generated by an educational system that models behavior that is designed to avoid injuring feelings.

The truth is that there *is* good and there *is* bad. They can be judged by their consequences. Good produces beneficial consequences and bad produces destructive consequences. You must judge the good and bad based on the fruit it produces, and not on whether or not everyone is doing it.

An ever increasing concern in the United States is pornography usage by those following incorrect principles. The subsequent consequences usually lead to serious addiction. Consider the following statistics. Are you aware of the fact that pornography revenue is larger than:

- The revenues of the top technology companies combined of Microsoft, Google, Amazon, eBay, Yahoo!, Apple, Netflix and Earthlink

- The combined revenues of ABC, CBS, and NBC

- All combined revenues of all professional football, baseball, and basketball franchises.

Time Statistics

Every second:
$3,075.64 is spent on pornography,
28,258 Internet users view pornography,
and 372 Internet users type adult search terms into search engines.

Every 39 minutes:
A new pornographic video is created in the United States.[32]

---

[32] http://familysafemedia.com/pornography_statistics.html#anchor2

The size of the industry world-wide is $97.1 billion with $13.3 billion being spent in the United States, alone. Adult videos generate revenue of $20 billion, escort services $11 billion, magazines $7.5 billion, sex clubs $5 billion, phone sex $4.5 billion, child pornography $3 billion, cable/pay per view $2.5 billion, and the Internet $2.5 billion and growing.

The Internet contains more than 4.2 million pornographic websites (12% of total websites). The average age of first exposure to pornography is 11 years old. A breakdown of male versus female visitors to pornographic sites is 72% male to 28% female, with 10% of adult respondents admitting to sexual addiction. Sexual addiction is increasing world-wide because of poor choices being made. Do these choices bring good consequences? They end up destroying relationships and enslaving the partaker, not to mention wasting an enormous amount of precious time.

Another big lie is that we don't need to worry about the future, and that we should focus on the short-term rather than the long-term. Many people today, whether youth or corporate executives, have bought into this philosophy. They tend to think about the present rather than the future, and that having a good time or meeting quarterly earnings projections is more important than having a reputation for honesty and fair dealing. This is the thinking that prompts us to use credit freely and place ourselves into debt rather than wait until we can pay cash. Pop-up ads and other enticements abound in the short-term to entice us to those Internet sites that are titillating and sensuous rather than to long-term committed relationships. When people abuse alcohol, drugs, or participate in pornography they only think of themselves.

Consider this example from the business world. Corporations used to do all they could to build market share for their companies. Market share is a long-term concept that entails the percentage of the total sales of a given type of product or service that is attributable to a given company. Now, in the business world, frequently the emphasis is on quarterly earnings per share or meeting a quarterly or short-term target. Unfortunately, when maximizing quarterly earnings becomes the goal, business executives engage in all kinds of earnings gamesmanship. Employees become assets that can be fired and hired at will rather than people who need to be nurtured and invested in. Sometimes, firms commit fraud to make their short-term results look better than they really are. Consider the following quote from a $3 billion fraud case.

> *"The company committed fraud by overstating its net income by approximately $3 billion. The overriding motivation was the pressure to ensure that the company always met Wall Street's growing quarterly earnings expectations for the company. The company's management knew that meeting or exceeding these estimates was a key factor for the stock price of all publicly traded companies and therefore set out to ensure that the company met Wall Street's targets every quarter regardless of the company's actual earnings . . . management improperly inflated the company's operating income by more than $500 million before taxes, which represented more than one-third of the total operating income reported by the company. The participants in the illegal scheme included virtually the entire senior management of the company, including but not limited to its*

former chairman and chief executive officer, its former president, two former chief financial officers and various other senior accounting personnel. In total, there were over 20 individuals involved in the earnings overstatement schemes.

As an example, in the first quarter, the chief accountant was asked to "cook the books" by 62 million. The chief accountant was skeptical about the purpose of these instructions, but he did not challenge them. The mechanics were left to the chief accountant to carry out. The chief accountant created a spreadsheet containing seven pages of fictitious journal entries which he had determined were necessary to carry out the CFO's instructions.

If we focus on the short term, we can be discouraged from getting an education, from preparing to be fathers and mothers, from learning how to work, from saving and being industrious, and from having ethical and moral values.

Another big lie is that we should be selfish rather than selfless, or that we should focus only on ourselves and not on others. If we think only of ourselves, it can ruin marriages, relationships, and cause us to be greedy. It can keep us from serving other people, from following the Golden Rule, and from feeling good about ourselves. It can destroy trust and self-respect. Also, since selfish people tend to be more discouraged than those who focus on others, they will likely feel self-pity and be depressed. It is when we reach out to serve others than we experience true happiness.

True joy is derived from serving others. This is especially true in marriages. If you are selfless you will always want to serve your spouse, and he or she will always want to serve you. Your marriage will be flourish and be a wonderful experience. If, instead, you focus only on yourself, you can make your marriage the most miserable experience possible. It is when marriage partners or individuals in a marriage become selfish that they put their marriages at risk.

From what has been published about post-war Iraq, it has become quite obvious that Saddam Hussein and his two sons, Ude and Kusei, were very selfish individuals. They only thought of themselves and their own needs. They took advantage of others to satisfy their own lusts and desires, even to the point of killing people when they wouldn't acquiesce to their demands. It is said that Ude would take 12 year old girls off the street to satisfy his lusts. When he desired a particular young lady, he would often have her boyfriend executed. Instead of being selfless, these individuals had become selfish to the extreme measure. They sought happiness in a place where it can never be found--in evil doing.

All of these lies are based on the big lie that the Law of the Harvest has somehow been suspended and does not apply. Don't buy into that falsehood. It is still in full force.

Since everything in the universe is ruled by law, it is possible to predict outcomes. There are many predictable outcomes. Research can predict the outcome of unprotected sex, recreational drug usage, drunk driving, smoking, etc. All of these actions have statistical outcomes which can be predicted.

The Law of Justice

The Law of Justice is a basic law, which simply stated is: Whenever a certain act is engaged in, a set penalty is enforced. It is a natural part of human life to demand justice. We have designed sophisticated systems to dispense justice. There seems to be confusion, however, relating to this law. Many people think it is unfair or unjust if someone who breaks the law suffers the consequences attached to the law. This is errant thinking and shows confusion between mercy and the law of justice. It is never unjust for someone who is aware of the law and breaks the law to suffer the consequences of the law.

The Law of Justice is related to the Law of the Harvest. Where there is no law, there is no justice and there is no penalty. This is true as a matter of definition. A law, to be understood, must be stated in terms of action and consequences. If you perform X, you will get Y. When people agree to abide by a law, it is justice if they suffer the consequences attached to the law. If someone takes your property, for example, it is just that he be forced to repay you. If a third party is willing to reimburse you for your property, then that third party can show mercy to the offender and justice can still be achieved.

If law is not enforced, and the structure of an organized society is lost, justice is not administered. If there is no system for the administration of justice, our sense of justice drives us to revenge, a negative and completely different concept.

**Acting upon correct and true principles
always leads to positive results.**

The Law of Action

The Law of Action can be stated as whenever there is an action, there is a result or consequence of the action. Even though it is merely movement, there is a measurable consequence. In a scientific definition, for every action there is an equal and opposite reaction. An act is the outward expression of inner will.

The Law of Preparation

Simply stated, the Law of Preparation declares that there are prerequisites to creation or achievement of any meaningful result. If you fail to plan, you plan to fail. To create a painting, you must first assemble the materials required and visualize the result. This applies in any other area of life, as well.

The Law of Honesty

The Law of Honesty can be stated as effective action takes place only when you are dealing with the real facts. If you are acting based on errant facts rather than the real facts, you will not receive the expected result.

The Law of Forgiveness

Forgiveness is a prerequisite for further action in a forward direction, whether it be self-forgiveness or the forgiveness of others. We move toward our focus. If we are placing our focus on a past event that physically or emotionally wounded us, we cannot move forward with our lives. I would recommend a book by Michael Schlappi entitled *Shot Happens* with the subtitle *I Got Shot, What's Your Excuse?* to see how forgiveness allows us to move forward with our own lives.

The Law of Faith

Faith is the first principle of action. The exercise of faith precedes any action. Lift your hand high above your head. The thought process that you took just before you lifted up your hand, is the process of faith. We open our mouth and speak because we first had faith that we could do so. Though it is difficult to perceive, we never act without faith.

The Law of Love

Love is the unifying principle of the universe. This law is typified by the willingness to sacrifice oneself for another person or group of people, because of an affection that one feels toward that person or group. Love is the most powerful of the inducements to action. Indeed, there are some actions that people will not ever take unless motivated by love. Love is looking out for another's needs before your own.

The Law of Cleanliness

There is the physical aspect of cleanliness, such as cleaning oneself or an area with disinfectant soap and water. My mother[33] explained the law of cleanliness as having a place for everything and everything in its place. Having our physical lives organized and clean guards against the spread of contaminates and lost focus.

---

[33] Thelma Brunt (1910-1997), homemaker and teacher

The Law of Unity or Focus

There is power in concentrated pressure. Try having someone hold up an 8 x 11 piece of paper with their hands on each side. Then lay your hand flat against the paper and push gradually increasing pressure. How long does it take you to break through the paper? Now repeat the exercise by pressing with only one finger. Presto! The paper breaks easily because of the concentrated focus. We can only focus on one thing at a time and we move toward the accomplishment of our focus.

In the "enlightened" age of intellectualism, our society has largely misunderstood the importance of truth. Many would like you to believe that there is no truth, but that all statements of truth are relative. Attempts to teach any principle as truth are often met with liberal criticism. The relativists maintain that there are no truths, only individual perceptions. The error in this thinking is that you cannot deny the consequences. While we are always free to act, we are never free from the consequences of our actions. If we discover and understand truth–as a statement of action and consequence, we can use it to our advantage to affect our outcome–the consequences of our actions.

CHAPTER 12

THE INTEGRITY
BUILDING PROCESS

Love is the most powerful element.

No one knows you better than you. Do you love yourself? Do you respect yourself? Do you trust yourself? Do you believe in yourself? What is your self-image like? Capacity is built from within, and the foundation of all capacity is self-trust. Self-trust is developed based upon experience and integrity. Since it is a process, we can follow that process and achieve the desired result.

Do you ever look at someone and say, "How can that person achieve so much, and I can't?" The truth is that you can do much more than you are currently doing. You can expand your own capacity.

Making and Keeping Small Commitments to Yourself

*This above all: to thine own self be true, and
it must follow, as the night the day, thou canst
not then be false to any man.*

Hamlet – William Shakespeare

The timeless admonition from Shakespeare restates the basis for building integrity. You can implement a process in your life of making and keeping small commitments to yourself. At first, you will hardly notice the impact. Within a week or so you will notice that you start thinking of yourself as someone who does what he says he is going to do. In a month, you will start adding more commitments and you will find you have the capability to accomplish them. As time goes on, you grow in self-respect, you will *see* yourself doing and accomplishing more, you will have an increasing feeling of self worth, your attention will turn outward, and you will grow in public respect, public trust, and public acceptance. Your core values will become more obvious to you and those around you, which will continually reinitiate the cycle.

This is the pattern that successful people have used throughout time. It is a pattern of growing from grace to grace, learning line upon line, precept upon precept, walking the straight path, and being pure in heart.

1. Getting a Clear Visualization of What You Want

You can either find an existing process or design a process to follow to become what you want to be. You can achieve your individual, social, intellectual, physical, career or family goals. Before you can actually think about the process, identify what it is that you want in each of these areas. What do you want to achieve? What capacity or power do you want to possess to achieve those objectives?

Books are meant to be written in if they are truly to become a help and part of a person's internalization of principles. A book with reader notes in the margins can indicate involvement in the process and a desire for further action. Take some time to ponder and reflect on the following questions and then enter your basic personal goals in the box on the following page. There is only room to list them simply here, but they can be developed in depth.

(1)   What do you want to achieve?

(2)   What is your commitment?

(3)   What capacity or power do you want to possess to achieve those objectives?

Example 1

Goal: Always be on time

Commitment: Arrive 10 minutes early to any event.

Capacity Develop social capacity, learn more, and demonstrate respect for others.

Example 2

Goal: Lose 3 pounds in 3 weeks.

Commitment: Track calorie intake on Loseit! app and walk 20 minutes a day.

Capacity: Improved physical capacity, self-respect, and confidence.

My Personal Goals

Goal:

Commitment:

Capacity:

Goal:

Commitment:

Capacity:

Goal:

Commitment:

Capacity:

Goal:

Commitment:

Capacity:

Now challenge yourself. What do you really want? The best indicator of what you really want is what you already really have. This is what your actions to date have led you to. When you are questioned by a coach or mentor with the questions, "Why do you want that?" try to give an honest answer. It is more difficult than you may think. What would motivate you to take regular daily actions toward the achievement of what you say you want? If you are not willing to take the actions, if your fears overcome your will, if your rationalizations halt your progress, perhaps you do not really want what you say you want. You might not want it enough to earn it with your actions.

It may be helpful to take the time with a coach or mentor to get really clear on what it is that you actually desire.

2. Developing a Process by Learning and Implementing Correct Principles

Once you know what you are trying to accomplish, you must decide how you can accomplish it. This takes a little time and study. Look for an existing program that other people have used to achieve the same result. Be careful that you do not get hooked into a false association. Remember your mind can easily make false associations. Don't try to lose weight by taking a miracle pill. Strive to get an understanding of the natural laws that govern, and then find a program that uses and acknowledges natural law. Weight Watchers is an example of a program that works under natural laws, and you can personally observe success stories.

One wise grandfather always taught his family that you could become anything you wanted to become. An avid sportsman, he used the example of becoming a good fisherman. His instructions included sitting on the bank and observing someone who was catching a lot of fish.

He advised, "Don't do any fishing at the time; instead, just watch everything the successful fisherman does in great detail. Talk to him or her and ask them for assistance. Find out the steps they take from the time they get up in the morning on a fishing day to the time they clean, cook, and eat that fish!"[34]

In essence, you are discovering the laws that pertain to fishing. You are learning about correct principles—principles that, if implemented are calculated to produce a certain result. The same principle of learning from others exists in every other realm of life.

3. Breaking up the Process into Ordered Tasks

Nothing about the process has to be complex. The simpler process is the often the better process. In the foregoing example, you would return from the banks of the river with a hundred details. Your goal would be to organize those details into an orderly set of things to do. If there are skills that you need to develop, those tasks might be placed first in the process. In the fishing example, you may have to practice assembling fishing rods and tying knots before moving on to the actual process of fishing.

---

[34] Reflections from George Brunt (1875-1956); grandfather to author and prominent Idaho businessman.

4. Tasks vs. Commitments

A task is something we know should be done. A commitment is our personal assumption of the task. It is making the task our own. The power in the process comes from making and keeping commitments. Everybody's day is filled with tasks. The important element in building personal capacity is in the making of a commitment to live a law or principle. Doing tasks is insufficient. There are many laborers who perform tasks day in and day out. Many times they do not know why they are doing what they do. Most are doing so because someone of higher power has told them to perform the task.

Once you know what has to be done, you are still not finished. Many people make to do lists. That is a part of the process. However, you cannot make a commitment to do those tasks until you think through what the obstacles are that will hinder your performance, why they are there, and how you are going to remove them. A to do list can become the weapon you use to beat up your self-image if you are not careful. Do not move your tasks to your commitment schedule until you have cleared the obstacles to performance.

Resistance is one of the main forces available to us in the strength-building process. Think for a moment about how physical strength is developed. If you go to a gym and hire a personal trainer, they set you up on a program that will involve repetitive resistance. As your strength develops, your application of resistance will become greater and greater. You might start on a program involving three sets of various repetitive resistance exercises using a very low weight. As you follow through, you will be able to increase the weight and become stronger and stronger. Your capacities to run, jump, and participate in both sports and physical work will increase and you will have greater abilities to serve others and your self-respect will increase.

Power in any of the other areas of life is developed much in the same way as physical strength. Repetitively overcoming resistance through commitment develops emotional strength, financial strength, social strength, mental strength, and spiritual strength.

Self-denial is the practice of resisting something of value in exchange for something of greater value.

In a society significantly influenced by the hedonistic view of self-gratification, we have lost much our understanding of the value of self-denial. Every time you make a decision in life you are practicing the art of self-denial. Life is a series of decisions and those decisions determine your outcome. When you decide what you want to do, you are also, by implication, deciding what you do not want to do. By selecting one activity you are eliminating several other activities. Knowing what you do not want is as important than knowing what you want. Resisting what you want in exchange for something that you want even more gives you the strength to obtain what you really want.

The power of being committed to doing what is right can overcome the perceived pressures and opportunities in life that cause us to compromise our integrity. Differentiate between tasks and long-term goals. If you do not keep your long-term objectives in mind, there is always a risk that you will get caught up in your short-term tasks—and then you are in danger of missing the forest for the trees.

This has been happening in corporate America in many ways. With shorter time frames, priorities are different and relationships and alliances become less important. The number one priority in corporate America used to be to build market share–which is a worthy long-term goal. Now, often the number one priority is to meet Wall Street's   quarterly earnings per share forecasts, a short term goal.

In short-term thinking, relationships and consequences of questionable or brief relationships become less important. When relationships are viewed as long-term, you would never do anything to harm another person, because it is harder to rationalize bad actions.   Many problems faced by corporate America and its employees are related to the total absence of long-term motivation. The average corporate executive today changes jobs every five years. Young men, analysts on Wall Street who predict corporate earnings, often have a greater impact on jobs, corporate results, and management decisions than do solid correct principles.

One seasoned executive of a public company emphatically told his staff, "I am not going to let some snot-nosed twenty-eight year old kid on Wall Street run my company."

This leader put long-term success over short-term driven results by ignoring the 'streets' short term expectations. He was committed to the long term view.

Narrowing the field to the tasks you actually want to commit to perform is one of the most important steps in developing greater capacity. You are much more likely to follow through and meet your commitment if you have recognized the relative values of each course of action, studied the long term result, and made a decision denying or cutting off the less acceptable actions. This means you must repetitively resist several courses of action. If you follow through and do what you have committed to do, your integrity will increase. As you have more trust and confidence in yourself, you will make and keep even greater commitments. If you continue in the course, the day will come when you can accomplish anything utilizing this formula—a day when you have perfect integrity and unlimited capacity.

5. Removing the Obstacles

Once you identify what the tasks are, you need to understand what the obstacles to performing those tasks are. Obstacles are usually related to the fear/benefit ratio or the pain and pleasure associated with what must be done. Getting clear on this ratio in your mind is essential to progress. You must think through the steps to accomplishing each task. What needs to be done beforehand? As an example, if you are working on a social value of keeping in closer contact with an expanded circle of friends, and you have developed a process of sending birthday cards and having a monthly telephone conversation with each of them, you must first identify those people, and get their telephone numbers, addresses, schedule time etc. Remove the obstacles that might prevent you from accomplishing your stated tasks.

6. A Written Plan

Describe the process in its simplest terms in writing. This will help you remember the process, follow through with it, and make it easier to teach to others. Only about 3-5% of people have a written plan to achieve their goals. Studies have shown that 3% of Harvard Masters of Business graduates make 10 times more than the other 97% combined due to their habit of writing down their goals and the plan to accomplish their goals.[35]

Why is a written plan so powerful? One reason is that a written plan keeps us focused on our goals and the action steps necessary to accomplish them. It is the most important step in following through with the actions required achieve the consequences you desire. We often resist writing out our plans and commitments due to our fear of failure or our other rationalizations. When we write our goals and plans down, we refine them, and that process adds focus, forcing us to think about the time and effort it will take, what resources are available, and what obstacles to overcome.

7.   The Commitment Process

Now that you know what you are going to do, how you are going to do it, and you have cleared the obstacles to performing it—and only when you have done these things—you are ready to make your commitment. This is a promise to yourself that you will accomplish your goal. Begin by committing and performing with exactness the first task in the process. In the fisherman example, it might be committing to read a book about fishing. One of George Washington's primary virtues was "diligence". Diligence is a constant and earnest effort to accomplish what is undertaken; it is the persistent exertion of body or mind. We must commit to diligence.

---

[35] http://sidsavara.com/personal-productivity/why-3-of-harvard-mbas-make-ten-times-as-much-as-the-other-97-combined

8. Calendaring Performance

When you are ready make a promise to yourself, schedule the performance on your calendar. This forces you to set aside the time you need to do it. Time is really just the measure between events. Any event takes time. One of the biggest mistakes people make in not keeping promises they make to themselves is not setting aside the time. If you dedicate a slot of time for the task, you are more likely to accomplish it. Accomplishing the task and keeping the commitment is key to building self-trust, self-respect, and self-esteem. Following the process described in this book gives you the best possible chance of building those results into your life.

9. Recording Performance – Keeping a Journal

Our memories are very short! Keeping a record of the commitments we make and keep helps us remember who and what we are. It is a vital step in the process. By embarking on the process of building personal capacity in your life, you are taking personal responsibility for each area of your life. By keeping a journal of your commitments and performances, you are taking personal accountability for each area of your life. The combination of responsibility and accountability is essential. In fact, you cannot take responsibility without accountability. Think of yourself as the steward over the time allotted to you in your life.

The Integrity/Capacity Model

Why Does the Integrity/Capacity Model Work?

The Integrity/Capacity model works by its very definition. It is the process of identifying what the steps are for the desired result, overcoming the resistance, and following those steps.

The reader should take time to study and process the model of the diagram on the following page. If you gain knowledge by identifying the necessary steps and the pertinent laws that apply to the process, and actually perform the necessary actions to accomplish the goal, then the desired results will follow!

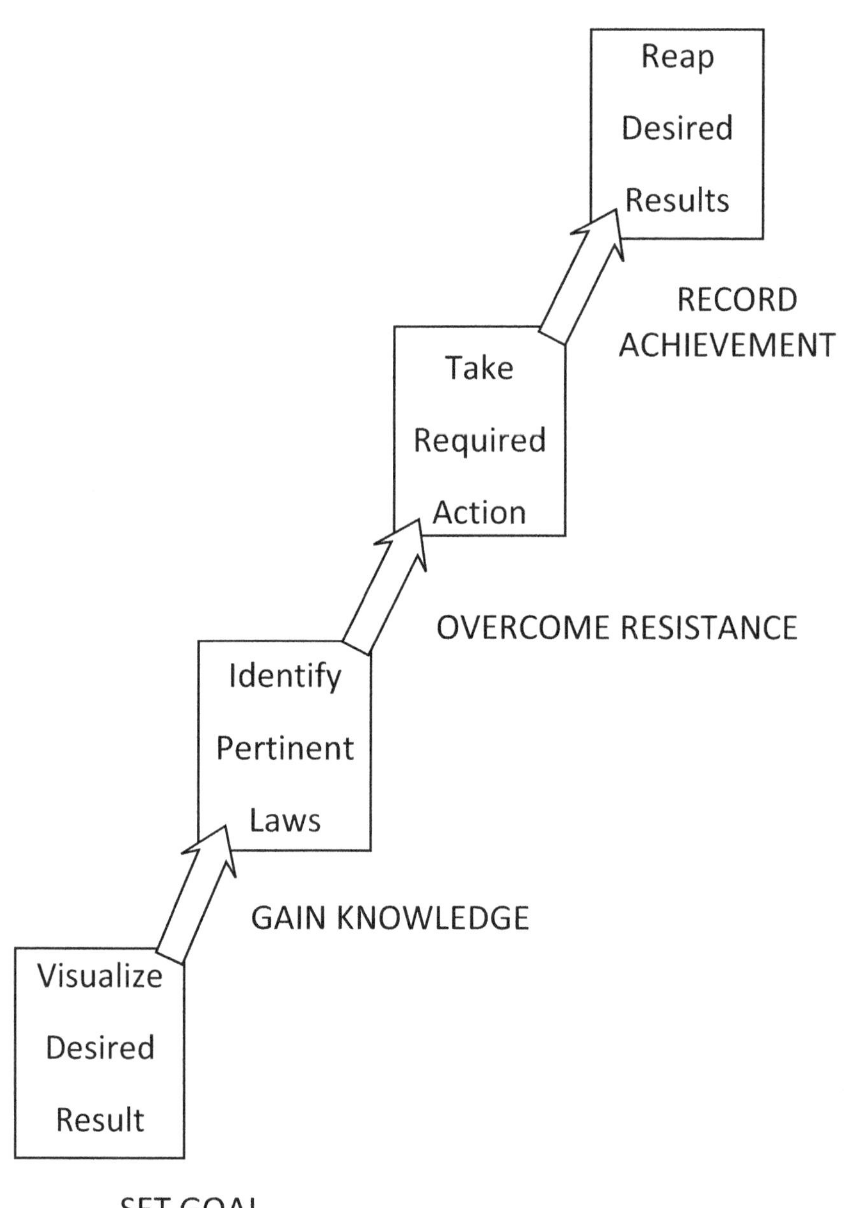
Reap
Desired
Results
RECORD
ACHIEVEMENT
Take
Required
Action
OVERCOME RESISTANCE
Identify
Pertinent
Laws
GAIN KNOWLEDGE
Visualize
Desired
Result
SET GOAL

CHAPTER 13

BUILDING
CORPORATE
CAPACITY

**"In looking for people to hire,
you look for three qualities:
integrity, intelligence, and energy.
And if they don't have the first,
the other two will kill you."**

— Warren Buffet
CEO, Berkshire Hathaway

Recently, we have seen some major failures in stewardship and the accounting for that stewardship. In the last ten years, news stories have reported about companies such as Enron, WorldCom, Tyco, Global Crossing, Adelphia, Quest,

Xerox, Bernard L Madoff Investment Securities LLC, and others. It is alleged that the stewards or executives of these companies weren't honest and their accountability was flawed. As a result, millions of people have lost billions of dollars in portfolios and retirement accounts. In fact, poor stewardship accounting led to the demise of one of the largest CPA firms, Arthur Andersen.

During the fallout of Enron's bankruptcy, Andersen ran an ad that their firm would do what was right. They were trying to rebuild consumer confidence in their accounting firm, but it was too late. While Andersen was attempting to pick up the pieces of their business, Paul Volcker, former Federal Reserve Chairman, presented a plan for a restructuring of Andersen so that they would have a chance of surviving this incident. Andersen did eventually agree to the restructuring, but it was too late to save the firm. [36]

In March 2009, "Bernie" Bernard Madoff pleaded guilty to eleven federal felonies and admitted to turning his wealth management business into a massive Ponzi scheme, resulting in the fraud of billions of dollars. There have been other such Ponzi schemes that have defrauded countless numbers of trusting investors.

At the core of any company are the people who work there. People are any corporation's greatest resource. Success or failure is not determined by anything done by the corporation. In fact, a corporation is a legal fiction. It is a fiction devised to solve two problems associated with private enterprise. The first solution that a corporate structure provides is a clear-cut mechanism for attracting investment capital. Investors can provide capital to people who, in turn, issue stock certificates to the investors as evidence of their participation. The second

---

[36] "Arthur Andersen and Enron: Positive Influence on the Accounting Industry," by Todd Stinson. faculty .mckendree.edu

solution is to provide limited liability for the people who invest in the corporation. Investors are held liable only to the degree of their investment.

The idea that a corporation can act outside of its people is irrational. Only people can advance the business, only people can make decisions, only people can fulfill commitments. A corporation cannot have capacity other than the capacity of its leadership and its workers. To increase the capacity of a corporation, it is necessary to increase the capacity of its individuals. This can be accomplished in two ways: hire more employees or increase the capacity of existing employees.

Management Versus Leadership Models

The way a corporation is managed has a profound effect on its ability to unleash the capacity of its people. If the top leadership has a view that people are to be managed, there will be automatic restrictions in capacity, and therefore in the result achieved. This was the view of most of the industrial managers of the past century. Empowerment, referring to a late twentieth century move to give power to individuals within an organization, was a dirty word to many people who ran corporations. They didn't want workers thinking or spending time developing strategies for improvement. That was a task for senior management. This is an example of an irrational fear. Executives only wanted a specific service from workers—a minimum duty performed in accordance with closely-controlled instructions. This is the management model. Using this model a corporation could never reach a capacity greater than what was possessed by its managers. Integrity was not a big issue, because there was only a certain minimum level of capacity required.

If top leadership has the view they are leading a team of contributors toward the accomplishment of mutual goals, the scenario is completely different. This is known as the leadership model. Empowerment is the objective under this model, and the capacity that can be tapped is unlimited. Senior managers in the leadership model serve as role models, motivators, listeners, teachers, cheerleaders and mentors. Employees become innovators, strategists and enablers. They find ways to help the organization achieve its objectives faster and more economically than management model executives could ever imagine. It only makes sense that the people closest to the challenges, in any area, would be the people with the best solutions to those challenges.

Most corporations in existence today still adhere to the management model. They invite consultants in to present seminars and speak about the leadership model. They sometimes use the word "empowerment" in their speeches, but they are afraid to let go of the reins; they are afraid to turn their back to the bull. Talk of empowerment is a frustration to employees, who clearly see the value of empowerment, but unfortunately, do not see the implementation Employees hear the talk, but do not see the walk. Why? Integrity is missing.

Remember integrity is the integration of correct principles. Senior management is the role model in this regard, demonstrating they have incorporated correct principles in their own lives and leadership style. The most important job of the executive is to identify, model, and teach the correct principles by which they expect employees to govern themselves.

An important lesson is learned from the phrase, "Behavior is born of belief, belief is born of doctrine, and the quickest way to influence behavior is to teach true doctrine."

This saying has a profound impact when pondered. Belief is the integration of doctrine, and people tend to act in accordance with their beliefs. Actions pronounce beliefs far better than words. If you help employees integrate correct principles, they will act in accordance with those principles. Keep in mind that correct principles are statements of cause and effect or laws. Once employees overcome false rationalizations, and truly integrate correct principles, they will act on those principles and the increase in results will be exponential. This is accomplished in an environment where corporate leaders model integrity.

Moral development researchers maintain that one develops honesty through a combination of proper modeling (example) and labeling (teaching and training). When either of these is absent, or when inappropriate modeling or labeling is present, people will be less honest. Unfortunately, bad modeling makes up most of the news we read and watch on television. Families who used to provide most of the honesty labeling are now spending less and less time together. The result is that many people working in business have developed situational rather than absolute ethics.

Companies that used the management model are not looking for input from the rank and file. Such companies have a very difficult time taking any action at all. Employees are always afraid to do the right thing for fear that it will cross some management decision. Management is often wallowing in self-deception. Customer satisfaction surveys reflect the dismal job they are doing, but the management team falsely excuses the poor performance, blaming imaginary factors outside of their control. These companies tend to have goals of increasing customer satisfaction or quality processes from a 45% level to a 55% level. Leadership model executives would never be satisfied with this result, and would be taking actions to achieve a 99% -100% level of quality or satisfaction.   There is a strong correlation between a lack of integrity and a lack of capacity to achieve strong results.

One company made a conscious decision to lie to its customers regarding the delivery date of its new products. There were several rationalizations for this behavior.

"All of our competitors shade the truth respecting delivery dates," or "we will not win the bid if we tell them the true delivery date," were common rationalizations.

Employees who were involved in the process were sickened by the prospects mandated by management to falsely insert delivery dates in the bid responses. What were the results? The company successfully won the bid, but at some point, had to inform the customer that the anticipated delivery date would not be met. More lies were told about why the date would be missed and the customer became very dissatisfied, because they had wasted time and resources based on promised delivery dates. Trust was lost. New promised delivery dates were received with skepticism, and for good reason. Management still failed to disclose the true delivery date, instead opting for an interim date they anticipated would be more palatable for the customer. Then, as that date approached, they chose to reveal a new interim delivery date closer to what they knew all along was in keeping with reality. The customer became totally disaffected as their anticipatory costs continued to mount and their trust in the vendor company continued to decline.

Some employees implored management to be truthful about delivery dates even though they might lose a bid here and there, because in the long run, customers would respect them for their integrity, and forego business relationships with the other vendors who lied to them concerning delivery dates. The truthful company could become the long-term vendor of choice. The customer could effectively plan their promotions and product introductions around the delivery of the equipment, and enhance the odds of a successful launch. New projects would go to the trusted vendor. The capacity of both companies would increase.

Some years ago, the SEC raised a case against a company. It was a sleepy little old firm, just barely making it, when a new leader took charge. He said, "I'm going to make this a go-go company. Pretty soon, instead of EPS (Earnings per Share) of 10:1, it's going to be 40:1. We're all going to get rich."

In turning the company around, he brought in a group of high-powered people, and adopted a policy called NBO (New Business Opportunity). Essentially, for a manager that meant that 'you and I agree on what your goals are going to be for your division next year; then I leave you alone to manage toward those goals.' Implied in NBO was the idea that it was a fair goal to start with.

As it turned out, the leader leaned on managers at the start of the year and said, "Look, we're going to earn $1.90 a share next year. Your share of that is $.42."

As the year went along, periodic meetings took place. If a manager was not on target at $.42 a share quarterly, the manager was told, "If you are unable to find a way to manage that goal, we'll find someone else who can." This statement does not need to be repeated many times until that employee finds a way to manage toward his goals.

One of the ways the leader did this was to say, "Who cares when you cut the books off. I mean, a sale is a sale, right? Does it really matter whether we reach a little bit into next week and take some of the sales we ship next week and put it in this week? After all, it was all made during this month anyway."

So, one week stretched into two weeks, and two weeks into three, until eventually it wasn't too hard to say, "We know that customer is going to buy the product; let's book it now."

Consequently, the company managed toward their objectives rather than towards reality, until finally they were so far beyond reality that the company collapsed from its own weight.[37] Such compromising standards are what often results in litigation and ruins business and personal relationships.

Steps to Developing Corporate Integrity

1. Visualize the Goal

The first step in applying the processes described in this book for achieving integrity is to clearly visualize the result you are trying to obtain for your corporation. You cannot discover the laws (statements of cause and effect) that will get you to your destination, unless you define your destination. If you don't know where you are going, any road will get you there, but it may not ultimately be the route you want to go.

2. Determine to Implement Correct Principles in Your Organization

This requires a commitment to the non-rationalized truth, and can be expressed as "Bring me the good news fast, and the bad news faster!"

Management cannot react to bad news that is buried deep within the ranks. Many famous leaders never learned about the bad news, because they were too well-known for "shooting the messenger." How irrational is that?

---

[37] Albrecht, W. Steve, editor, "Ethical Issues in the Pratice of Accounting," South-Western Publishers, 1992, p. 24-25.

3. List All of the Correct Principles

Make an actual list of every correct principle that your team can come up with. Remember that a correct principle is stated as an "if-then" proposition. An example might be, "*If* we meet every customer concern within a 24 hour period, *then* their word-of-mouth advertising will increase our sales more than dollars spent on actual advertising."

State the list in systems language, i.e., the following list consists of ways to systematically involve more people in identifying and solving opportunities in any company:

1. Enhance two way communication between
    leaders and teams.
2. Facilitate regular group brain storming sessions.
3. Practice restating for better listening.
4. Instill a system for rewarding contribution.

4. Identify Actions that Must Done

Identify the actions that must be taken to achieve your vision in accordance with the principles that govern the systems you have identified in step three. What actually must be done? Break this down in detail and relate it to how it achieves the objective.

Ask critical questions. For example, identify what it would take to "meet every customer concern within a 24 hour period". Do you need new technological systems? What are your strengths? What are your weaknesses? How would you accomplish the goal and what is the order and priority?

Set no more than three strategic objectives and break those down into quarterly action steps that must be accomplished to achieve the strategic initiative.

5. Identify and Remove Obstacles

What will keep you and your organization from taking the actions you need to take? What are the fears, the false rationalizations, the things that will paralyze your organization from acting? Write these down on a whiteboard and develop a plan to overcome each obstacle.   This is a time for careful listening to your team. Everyone needs to believe and buy into the solution. They cannot just pay lip service to the goal. Every objection, fear, and concern must be carefully listened to and addressed to the satisfaction of each member of the team. Taking action requires faith, hope, courage, and determination.   If obstacles to taking action loom in anyone's mind, you can be defeated before you begin. You must evaluate your teams and make sure that you have critical thinkers who can overcome obstacles.

6. Write a Plan.

If you have a written plan you will be ten times more likely to accomplish the plan. Writing the plan out will help clarify each action step, identify the person responsible to take the action, and define what success looks like. The plan includes the time frames for taking action and the reporting accountability process. Written strategic objectives and written annual as well as quarterly action steps that must be accomplished make it possible to track and measure your own success. It streamlines the annual reviews for each employee and makes it clear which employees are succeeding in supporting the company vision.

7. Take Action

Only actions have consequences. Even if you know what your company vision is and what steps are necessary to achieve the vision without actions, you will not achieve your vision. External forces sometimes deflect the plan and you will be trying to figure out why you have not achieved what you intended. The purpose of strategic planning is not to have a fancy plan, but to achieve the results intended. If you have a documented, thoughtful plan showing the actions to be accomplished and identify who will accomplish the actions and when, managing the process is simplified. You and your employees will have the tools required to measure their success.

8. Document.

One of the most important actions is to "return and report." This develops institutional knowledge that can be used to refine the strategic process within the company. Three questions are critical:

1. What actions worked?

2. What actions did not work?

3. Why did those actions work or not work?

This is the process for developing and acting in accordance with truth. If you were mistaken in the correlation between action and result (the Law), you can adjust and try other actions until you discover the truth. Once you know the truth you can always act in accordance and get the result you intend to achieve. Since corporations and business are not always run by the same employees, documentation assists upcoming management in taking the right actions and avoiding repetition of past failures.

9. Experiment and Modify

If what is being done is not working, experiment and change current actions in order to achieve better results.

Success in a corporation is systematic. Determine what systems work best to achieve your objectives, and then document and follow those systems–always looking for ways to improve or enhance the system. There is a system for building a great culture, a system for getting leads on customers, a system for achieving profitability, etc. Get a clear direction, discover and define the system, and then train and sustain. Train your people on the system, what it is designed to achieve, and what actions to make it happen. Then sustain the system by constant reinforcement. Once systems define your success, it is easy to consistently replicate that success by following the system.

CHAPTER 14

BUILDING MARITAL CAPACITY

**"Passion is the quickest to develop,
and the quickest to fade.
Intimacy develops more slowly,
and commitment
more gradually still."**

-Robert Jeffrey Sternberg

The family is the fundamental unit of society. The foundation of the family is the marriage relationship. Together, a married couple can have far greater capacity than either can have alone. However, just as with an individual, a corporation, or a nation, the full capacity of a marriage can only be reached through the development of greater integrity. No matter what stage of life you are in, there are steps you can take each day that will result in greater integrity, and therefore, greater capacity for your marriage.

A low integrity marriage has very limited capacity and a lot of challenges. The marriage relationship is an exclusive relationship. The partners vow to each other they will be true and faithful to each other. This vow precludes any other relationship on the same emotional, spiritual, financial, social, or physical levels as the relationship enjoyed with one's spouse. Certainly it is obvious, that when either partner is secretly or openly choosing to break this vow, in any area, the capacity of that relationship decreases.

The minute someone cheats on their spouse, he or she begins the rationalization process leads to the destruction of the marriage, and diminishes the capacity both of the individuals and their children. We all want to think of ourselves as being good. We tend to judge ourselves by our intentions and our spouses by their actions. 'If my spouse was more attentive, I never would have had to seek attention elsewhere,' is a common rationale. We rationalize that the spouse is bad and we are good. We stop communicating and hold back physically, financially, socially, emotionally, or spiritually.

If you ever find yourself holding back on your spouse in any of the foregoing areas, there is room to improve your integrity, and, therefore, the capacity of your marriage and family. Every married person who is reading this will be somewhere on the following continuum. Where do you fit in?

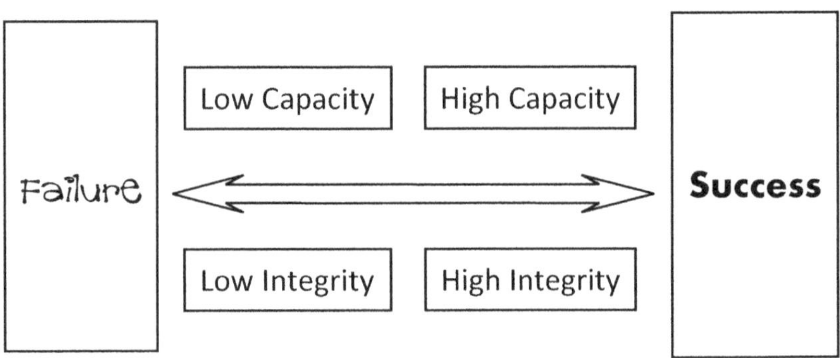

If you find yourself on the left side of the continuum, how can you move forward towards higher marital success? If you desire to have a high capacity relationship in your marriage, you can by increasing your integrity. A young couple does not immediately have a high capacity marriage merely from reciting vows. In interviews with dozens of married couples, a uniform view is that marriages improve with time by facing challenges and growing together.

The integrity standard for marriage is complete fidelity.

Marital capacity grows in an ordered progression, as expressed in Levels I-V in the following descriptions:

Level I

The first level is to live by a standard of physical fidelity. This is a promise between a man and a woman to the effect that their physical relationship is a special, personal relationship only between them, and that they will have no sexual relationships with anyone other than their spouse. This is, perhaps, the easiest in relative terms of the areas to perform a perfect achievement. It is not always easy, because there is a great pull from outside sources that attempt to undermine this commitment. It is the breach of this promise that destroys so many families and marriages. This base line commitment of physical fidelity is the foundation of capacity in a marriage.

Level II

The second level is to share equally in material things. "All that I have is yours," is a common part of many marriage vows. Many people have a more difficult time actually living this commitment with complete fidelity. Basic human selfishness presents a strong pull. Often the spouse that brings in the most financial support for the marriage wants to dictate how that money should be spent, or actually individually spends the money in ways that are not agreed upon in advance. Financial fidelity requires open communication and cooperation.

Level III

The third level is social priority. This is a promise between the couple that they will have no social relationships that have a higher priority than their social relationship with each other. Your spouse should never have to put on a "mask" in social settings.

Dr. Phil, a prominent television personality, once put it this way: "If your spouse was in a room with 1000 other women, she should know in her heart that none of them are being treated as well as she is, even behind closed doors."

Marriages are bombarded by externalities. These externalities are things that come in from the outside and create problems (even good things can cause problems, if excessive). Integrity in a marriage means that we never let any of these externalities come between us and our spouse. Examples of some of those externalities, not listed in any order of cause, are listed as follows:

- Friends
- Conflicts of Interest
- Money
- Travel
- Sports and Hobbies
- Work
- Exercise
- Bad Habits
- Pets
- In-laws

Level IV

The fourth level is living by a standard of emotional fidelity. This is a promise that they will have no other emotional relationships that take precedence over their emotional relationship with each other. If you derive more emotional satisfaction from a game of golf with your buddies, hunting, playing Internet games with others, a chat with your best friend, etc. than from being with your spouse, you have some work to do. Agree to create an atmosphere of emotional safety and understanding.

Level V

The fifth level is the sharing of spiritual influences. This is a commitment to live lives of integrity in accordance with higher source principles. The fifth level requires the adoption of the previous four. Each level is a foundation for the next level; they build upon one another.

LEVELS FOR COMPLETE MARITAL CAPACITY

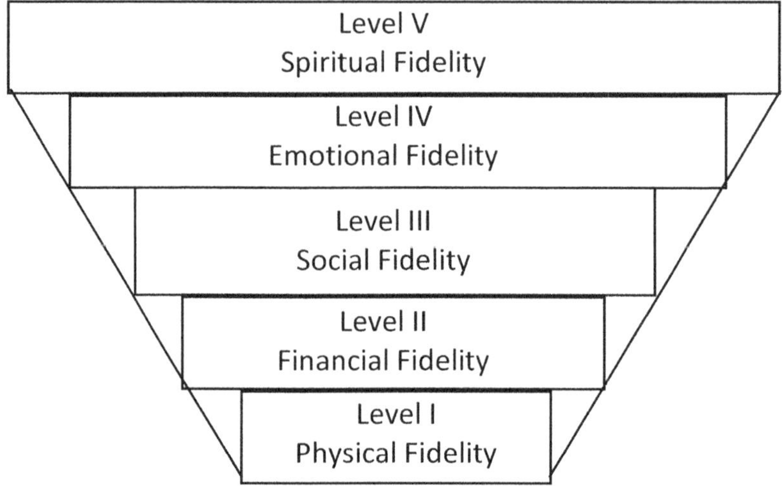

Notice the pyramid in the example is inverted. Growth is expansionary. There can be so much power and capacity in a marriage and in a family who has built and expanded their capacity through taking actions consistent with the correct principles of marriage in each of these areas. There is no satisfaction or security greater than that felt by a couple who have raised a family in such an environment.

True integrity in a marriage relationship means that we honor our spouse.

- When you honor something or someone, nothing is as valuable, important, weighty, or significant.

- Honor means that you change yourself, not others.
- Kindness is communicating through your actions that you honor someone, not just by what you say.
- If you honor someone, you never do anything behind his or her back (conflict of interest).
- If you honor someone, you would never hurt him or her intentionally, because you view the long-term relationship as preeminent.

Building Marital Integrity with Physical Fidelity

If you desire to increase your capacity in the physical area of your marriage, you may do so by visualizing the result you desire, identifying the truth about the physical relationship, overcoming the obstacles or resistance, committing, and never leaving out the final step–doing!

What is the result you desire? Most people desire a healthy, vibrant, committed, worry-free physical relationship with their spouse. There is a set of truths pertaining to the achievement of these goals and they are pretty simple. Complete physical, mental, and emotional fidelity between spouses is the formula for achieving a healthy, vibrant, committed, worry-free physical relationship. What are the obstacles? There are many! The good news is that they are all the result of the choices you make. As you resist obstacles, they will become easier to resist. The bad news is that if you do not, they will have power over you. Following are some obstacles that you must choose to resist:

- Selfishness
- Ego
- Pornography
- Foul Language
- Poor communications

What makes a person truly committed to carry through with their intentions?

"There's a difference between interest and commitment. When you're interested in doing something, you do it only when circumstance permit. When you're committed to something, you acccpt no cxcuses, only results."[38]

It is easy to say that we commit. It is more difficult to remain committed to your commitment. Commitment is evidenced by actions, not words. It is a constant course–a daily effort to make correct choices, and to resist the forces that pull you toward the obstacles. As with all truth, as with all laws, the result flows from the consistent doing. By definition, a law is a statement of the ingredients and processes required to achieve a certain result. No amount of mere thinking or even simply committing will achieve the result. The law must be obeyed, and there must be action in accordance with the law.

Building Marital Integrity with Material Fidelity

The same forces are at play in building fidelity in a marriage for each of the areas of life. A husband and wife who are on the same bandwidth regarding material things will have a distinct advantage. The absolute truth pertaining

---

[38] thinkexist.com/quotation/there-s_a_difference.../222268.html

to achieving the result of material fidelity is also easily stated: The husband and wife must agree on their financial and material requirements, and work together with complete candor and disclosure. The financial goals and situation of the family must be completely upfront and transparent and agreed upon by both spouses. The obstacles for achieving this result include, but are not limited to:

<table>
<tr><td>• Greed</td><td>• Instant Gratification</td></tr>
<tr><td>• Ego</td><td>• Lack of Interest</td></tr>
<tr><td>• Selfishness</td><td>• Lack of knowledge</td></tr>
<tr><td>• Debt</td><td>or Understanding</td></tr>
</table>

One man complained that his wife threw money out the back door as fast as he could bring it in the front door. This man never could accumulate savings, though he made an adequate income. His family never had the capacity to take vacations together, have a summer home, go to the best schools, have a worry-free retirement, or to have other options that a high capacity marriage enjoys. The truth is he never shared his financial situation with his spouse; they never agreed on what they needed or what they both were willing to do to achieve financial goals. In his mind, he was the provider. His ego would not let him include his spouse in the goals, the planning, or the program pertaining to their financial situation. His ego didn't allow him to include his wife in the goal-setting/budgeting process because he blamed her for the monetary challenges.

Material fidelity in marriage is crucial to the capacity of the family. In my own experience, early in our marriage we determined together what our material needs were going to be. It only made sense that if both spouses were committed to the plan, there would be a better chance of success Important factors affected the material requirements. Having one parent in the home to personally raise our children was a requirement of our material plans. My wife and I agreed that we would live on whatever amount we were able to earn in order for her to remain at home with the children. Remember, capacity is not measured in material or monetary terms alone.

In order to achieve greater capacity in our family, material sacrifices were made. This one decision, dictated by our desire to have a full-time mother in the home, gave our family greater ability to resist the obstacles to material success. The willingness to sacrifice makes the resistance to obstacles easier, and the resistance to obstacles makes living the laws that lead to positive results easier. As a result our family is financially independent and able to enjoy activities together.

Building Marital Integrity with Social Fidelity

Some might argue that social fidelity is not an important part of the marriage vow. If you find yourself making this argument, be open to the possibility that it is a rationalization designed to bring your principles in line with your conduct. When we follow laws, we bring our conduct in line with principles. It is a more difficult road but the only road that leads anywhere.

What do we mean by social fidelity? It is just as important as material fidelity. It is the development of a set of rules, determined together as spouses, which define what part of ourselves we will share with the world. It is a social plan for our marriage and our family, and it could vary between couples. Many marriages fail or end up in bitter acrimony because the marriage partners never think about, arrive at, or follow a social plan. What are the obstacles to building integrity in this part of your marriage?

Below are some possible obstacles:

- Never Developing a Set of Rules
- Old Friends
- New Friends
- Excessive Work Hours
- Excessive Civic/Church Duties
- Outside Hobbies or Clubs
- Sports Interests

With complete physical and marital integrity, adding social fidelity to the program will greatly enhance the capacity of the marriage. Imagine the result if you are both working a plan to contribute to others, to serve others, and to turn your focus outward. The greatest sense of self-worth, self-trust and self-respect come from serving other people. You comprehend their needs, their problems, their sadness, but also their appreciation for your assistance, their happiness, and their joy. This can enhance your sense of worth. It is true that we find our own lives when we lose them in the service of others.

We are not just single individuals developing our individual capacity; instead, we are married partners, often raising our families, serving in neighborhoods, communities, churches, and charities in addition to work. We are developing a new and greater type of capacity, which we are calling marital capacity.

We do not mean to imply that after marriage, we are bound to be social with only one person. Instead, after marriage, social interests should be pursued as a team with a designed set of rules which are mutually agreed upon and followed. An example of going against this principle is shown in a situation faced by one young couple. They were bright and beautiful individuals who seemed to be meant for one another. However, the husband maintained a Thursday night out with his old buddies. It was not an arrangement that his wife approved of. Just as a small crack in the surface of a space shuttle can lead to its break-up, it was clear that there was a dangerous crack in their marriage. The relationship eventually terminated largely based on the lack of social integrity.

Building Marital Integrity with Emotional Fidelity

Many marriages never achieve emotional fidelity. Imagine your marriage with both spouses committed to complete emotional fidelity. That means that neither one of you will ever withhold your feelings of admiration, acceptance, approval, devotion, love, support, and preference from your spouse. There would be no cruel criticism. Each spouse would put full commitment of the heart behind the outward commitments of mind and body. A marriage that has the complete heart of both spouses in it will have much greater capacity than any marriage with a partial-hearted commitment.

Visualize what that would be like . . . neither spouse would fear completely disclosing their confidences or weaknesses in such a relationship. The emotional support of each spouse would help the other see and overcome the obstacles they face. Even the physical relationship, often strained through the lack of emotional commitment and emotional withholding, would dramatically improve.

What are the laws that pertain to building emotional fidelity in a marriage? Emotional fidelity requires that each spouse put the feelings of the other spouse above their own feelings. It requires open and honest communication in an accepting environment. It requires a deeper appreciation.

There are university courses in art appreciation. An untrained eye will miss much of the deeper meaning presented by the artist by the use of detail, light, depth, color and other factors, including the history and purpose behind the particular art object. It is a similar deeper level of heartfelt appreciation that we must learn to have for our spouses. It is not just that we like our spouse, it is that we appreciate all the intricacies, histories, strivings, and devotions that make our spouse so much more than we ever imagined. If you do not know your spouse at this level, there is work to do.

What are some obstacles that make us hold back from achieving complete emotional fidelity? Some of them include:

- Selfishness
- Jealousy
- Fear
- Ego
- Resentment
- Outside emotional attachments

Building Marital Integrity with Spiritual Fidelity

Spiritual fidelity is different from emotional or social fidelity. When two people are of the same heart and mind, agreeing on a set of rules that embody all truth, they will be together on a journey that will lead them to full capacity, both as individuals and as a married couple. There is no magic here! No supernatural hocus-pocus is involved. Wherever we discover and follow truth, we will reap real results; otherwise we are just deceiving ourselves. Remember what truth is. It is what is.

There is nothing so foolish or futile than to resist what is. It is a statement of law. A law is an expression of a recipe, that when followed, consistently achieves a given result. When two people jointly discover and follow law, their capacity together will someday know no limits—given an unlimited life span. Of course, we know we do not have an unlimited life span. By its very definition, mortality implies that we each will experience a physical death. During the duration of our short span on earth, it is impossible for us to independently discover all the rules that effectively and consistently lead to good outcomes (laws). That is by no means evidence that the laws do not exist. In fact, all the evidence that we have indicates that laws exist in every sphere and system. We have made great advances in the past 150 years in discovering laws. Our discoveries have led to more discoveries, until we have come to realize that the more we know, the greater we realize our universe is full of laws left to be discovered. We knew little of the miniature universe of microns and atoms and quarks two hundred years ago. There are many systems that we are aware of, but we cannot yet explain.

Yet, one of the little oddities of human nature is that we seem to want to rediscover all the laws for ourselves. Parents delight when their children heed their counsel and the counsel of others whose life experiences can help them avoid paths that do not lead to good results. Yet we, as adults, are often victims of the same rationalizations and fears that lead our children into unproductive paths. We are not isolated here without counsel. Over the ages, we have been given several texts that teach us of history, of what worked for the people that preceded us on this planet, and what lead to futility, to their decline, or even to their destruction. We also have the lessons they learned and what led them to success, discovery, and happiness. Several of these texts proclaim they are of divine origin, revelations from a higher source, even from a loving Heavenly Father who desires the best outcome for His children. The truth remains the truth no matter where we learn it. The laws are in place in every sphere. Why should every married couple try to discover these laws on their own, by chance? Why should they teach their children to do so? We should each try to accept truth from every reliable source. It can be tested. If it bears fruit or results in a good benefit consistently, it works.

I am not advocating that anyone should blindly follow a dogma or doctrine to achieve spiritual growth. If it is not working, stop doing it and seek for something more. "Question everything,' the slogan from the 60's, is valid. We should question everything to be sure that it leads to a good outcome or effect, and if it does we need to overcome the obstacles that stand in our way. If we are going to question, we should question everything, not just what's comfortable for us. That is the only way to avoid self-deception. In doing so, we must remember to obtain and apply an answer. Constant questioning without decision-making, applying, and testing leads us to no results.

It is clear that marriage itself is a higher law designed to lead to a fullness of happiness, where couples can work together to become selfless and live the laws of life. Get on the same page with your spiritual values, the page of truth, whatever the source, and your marriage will become dramatically stronger and happier. Having similar moral and religious values can give your marriage a strong head start, but they must be tested and applied to have any real impact. Believing causes us to do; doing causes us to grow.

One of the truly unique aspects of the marriage relationship is that we can help each other in a safe environment. We can help each other see with another set of eyes what is working and what is not working; we can hear with another set of ears what is working and what is not working. The recognition of weakness (things we do that do not work) is the beginning of strength.

CHAPTER 15

BUILDING INTELLECTUAL CAPACITY

**It is not how smart you are,
but how you are smart.**

How can we build our intellectual capacity? Intellect has always been a subject that has caught my interest. Is it a natural ability? Can it be improved? These are questions that are not contradictory. They can both be answered with a "yes," but I have not always known that.

Like most kids, the world of learning was challenging and fascinating for me. In grade school I had teachers that convinced me that I was smart. I excelled in their class rooms and thought I was smart, witty, and talented. In the first part of 7th grade I continued to believe that I could keep up with the other kids intellectually. Then we moved and I went to a new school and was placed in an Algebra class. At the previous school I had not learned anything about Algebra. On the first day of class my teacher announced that we were going to take a test that would separate the wheat from the tares. The test was designed to see how much algebraic knowledge we already possessed. To my dismay, I received a very low score on the test. Many of my fellow students, who were not transferring in from another school, had received a solid foundation in Algebra, having taken a pre-algebra the first semester. I had not.

The teacher then did an interesting thing. She had all of the "wheat" sit on one side of the class and all of the "tares" sit together on the other side of the class. I still remember the chair I was sitting in when she made this humiliating announcement. I did not have to move as I was already sitting on the "tare" side of the room. She then proceeded to teach to the students categorized as *Wheat* and told the *Tares* that we could follow along the best we could.

From that day forward for many years I was convinced that I was not capable of keeping up with the "smart" kids. I turned out to be an average student in high school and an average student for my first years in college. A college counselor told me that I was so weak in mathematics that I should not pursue a college education, but should seek a trade school. I chose to stay in college and took a remedial math course to prepare for the basic requirements in math.   I was determined to learn mathematics. Even though I tried to take a math class each semester, my performance did not change too much until after I met my wife. I was complaining to her that I just was not as smart as other people in math.

She was shocked. She said, "Really?" Then she set me on the path to building intellectual personal capacity from which I have never turned back.

This counsel, this input from my wife, is really the basis for this entire book. She brought to my attention that I was weak in the area of studying. The recognition of this weakness was the beginning of my strength. She had me apply the process that has been discussed throughout this book. She convinced me that I was as smart as anyone, but that I just did not believe that I was, nor did I take the steps that those people took to achieve the level of performance that they were achieving. I first had to see the vision that I was as smart as the next guy. Once I realized this, I had to find out what the other people were doing who were out performing me. It turns out that they were studying more. Now people–parents, siblings, teachers etc. had always told me to study, but I did not catch the vision of what they were talking about. I did not believe that studying would benefit a tare like me. I took solace in the fact that I was adept socially and an excellent skier. I did not dream that I could compete at the intellectual level, but I knew that I could get by. I thought that studying only benefited the "smart" kids, the *wheat*. What my wife helped me to realize that day is that if I was achieving decent grades in college without studying, think what would be possible if I did study. She helped me see that I was "wheat."

Then I had to find out what to do. Luckily she knew. She told me that it is very simple. Just read every assignment, do every quiz, and review my notes three times. The first time she had me read for a general overview, the next time to pick out key points, and the final time to pick out what I thought the professor would ask. I got such good grades my final two years, after my wife's counsel, that I was able to get into a law school, do well there, pass the bar and spend a career in the field of law for the past 38 years. I thank God everyday for a wife who inspired me to be a better man, a man who began to believe, and then took action based on those beliefs, and reaped years of happy consequences.

You are probably thinking, "Is this the chapter on building marital capacity?" No, but it does illustrate the point.

Every system is governed by a set of laws. When we discover what those laws are and act in compliance with those laws, we will reap the consequences delivered by the system. This process of doing what we know we should be doing is the process of building integrity and we can do this in every aspect of our lives.

Do not accept the labels that others might want to place on you! There will be many people who are quick to judge and more than willing to place a label on you. Some people are so used to placing labels that they cannot help themselves. Even people who love us can be quick to label us. I wore the label of "tare" for far too long. Being labeled and accepting labels is commonplace. I have heard parents say, in front of their children, "Oh, this is my smart child," or" This is my pretty child," implying that someone else didn't get the brains or looks, etc. Conversely, parents may even label a child with negative labels when they say such things as, "Oh, he has such a temper!" Take care not to label others or wear negative labels others have given you.

Styles of Learning

Science has made great strides in discovering that we learn differently from one another and that we vary in strengths and skills. MI Cubed has developed a science around how people learn. It turns out that there are 7 learning types:

Verbal Linguistic:
Learns by studying books and listening to lectures

Spatial:
Learns by seeing things in proportion

Body Kinesthetic:
Learns hands-on by doing

Musical:
Learns in a sequential order

Math Logic:
Learns though understanding logic and equations

Intrapersonal
Learns by processing information on their own

Interpersonal:
Learns by discussing with a group of peers

Most people tend to have more than one learning style, but one is usually predominant. My personal learning style combines body kinesthetic and intrapersonal. It is not how smart you are, but it is all about how you are smart. Once you understand that you are smart, but just learn differently, you can learn whatever you want to learn. If you are interested in knowing your learning type you can take a simple online test at *www.micubed.com.*

It is tragic how many people believe that they are unable to learn or to develop intellectually. In reality, there are no limits to what we can learn, and no limits to our intellect. We can develop greater intellectual capacity. It has to do with discovering and living the laws of intellectual development.

CHAPTER 16
BUILDING
PHYSICAL
CAPACITY

**"The way to get started
is to stop talking
and start doing."**

-Walt Disney

There is no law that requires everyone to be a body builder muscle man or woman in order to maximize physical capacity. However, there is a law that states that what is not used diminishes and there are laws that govern maintaining your health.

There is a highway near my summer home in Idaho. When I was a young boy, it was the main highway to Yellowstone National Park. Thousands of cars would drive along this famous scenic route. When I became a teenager, a new highway was built. The old highway saw fewer and fewer cars. It began to diminish. Today there are parts of the old highway that are completely reclaimed by nature. This has happened just in my lifetime. Of course, a highway must be maintained to stay in pristine shape, but the minute it was not in regular use it began to diminish. The same is true with our physical bodies. The minute we cease to maintain them . . . the minute they are not regularly used and not regularly maintained, they begin to diminish. This is true with all materials in nature. It is a universal truth.

So what is the goal you might set regarding the condition of your physical body? What level of capacity do you see for yourself? Would you like to be capable of hard physical labor? Would you like to be able to keep up with your children or grandchildren? Would you like to be able to enjoy physical activities like hiking, running, sightseeing etc. with your spouse and family? Would you like to have the health and stamina to provide for your family's physical, emotional, and spiritual needs? There is definitely a correlation between the capacity to learn, love, and to leave a legacy and your own physical capability.

If you desire to develop greater physical capacity, what do you do? The first step is to imagine. You need to actually visualize in great detail exactly what you want to be like physically. Close your eyes and see yourself as you would like to be. What are you doing? Who are you doing it with? What are you wearing? What are the colors? Try this visualization exercise before you set goals.

The second step is to believe. It doesn't matter what kind of shape you are in now—if you do not believe you can become your vision, you will have difficulty achieving it. Believing comes before seeing.

Next comes the discovery. What are the laws that govern physical health? Scientific studies continually enhance understanding of the human body, but the basic laws still apply.

- Water is crucial to our health.
- Certain chemical substances are harmful to our bodies.
- Any substance can be harmful to our bodies in too high of quantities.
- Our bodies benefit from regular exercise.
- We need to control the intake and outflow of calories.
- Our bodies require a certain amount of sleep

Even with a basic understanding of these laws, many of us in the modern age of convenience, rationalize behaviors to the point that we get out of shape and become overweight. In this condition, our capacity is limited. We do not have the stamina and energy to contribute, participate, learn, love, serve, or leave a legacy for our posterity as we might desire. Why?

Let's explore some false beliefs and rationalizations. Media leads us to believe we can overindulge and become popular. The fast food commercial convinces us that super sizing provides us value. We associate sitting on the couch and watching TV with pleasure, and we associate work with pain.

Face it! We are fully capable of believing something that is false–even when we really know the truth. We will act on our beliefs–even our false, emotional level beliefs. To absolutely believe, we must accept not only with the brain, but with the heart and our emotions.

Belief in truth takes effort. It is easy to believe lies, but belief in truth requires sacrifice, effort and action. Believing in a falsehood often is passive. It usually does not require the same level of sacrifice, effort, and action.

The Bible says, "Therefore, to him that knoweth to do good, and doeth it not, to him it is sin"[39] Even in the secular sense if we know what to do to obtain a certain consequence, we must take that action or we will not enjoy the consequence.

The basic law governing physical health states that to properly maintain the health of the body, it must constantly be nourished with the proper nutrients, minerals and oxygen in order to enable its cells to function properly.

In an interview with Winn Claybaugh,[40] the author of *Be Nice, Or Else!,* he observed it is not the big decisions that influence our lives the most. It is the constant little decisions that have the most impact. It is not easy. If you are looking for easy, believe the lies and forgo the results. It takes practice. If you want to be in great physical shape, practice being in great physical shape. What? In the interview with Winn, he noted that at one low and unhappy point in his life one of his mentors told him to practice being happy. He thought, What? Then it dawned on him that at one time he could not play the piano. What did he do? He practiced playing the piano. Now, in my opinion, Winn is a concert level pianist. Why? Because he practiced doing what he could not do. Winn is also happy. Why? Because he practiced doing what he thought he could not do.

Most of us know a lot about the laws that govern physical health. Our governments have realized the importance to society of a healthy population, and have required the curriculum in our schools. Entrepreneurs have recognized the desire in most people to have good health and have developed training and programs to follow. We can continue to learn, but the state we are in is not due to our lack of knowledge, rather our lack of vision, belief,

---

[39] James 4:17

[40] Winn Claybaugh is a nationwide motivational speaker, author, and founder and co-owner (with John Paul DeJoria) of Paul Mitchell.

and our willingness to practice what we cannot do.

Sir Isaac Newton taught us an important and universal law when he observed that in the physical world for each action, there is an equal and opposite reaction. Another way of stating this law is that for every action there is a consequence. You cannot take action without getting a result. The reason why Winn Claybaugh teaches that it is the little daily decisions we make that count and not the large ones is because with each little decision we make on a daily basis we either do or do not take an action. If we take the action we will get a result. The cumulative effect of the actions we take or do not take will determine who and what we become, what we look and feel like, and what our capacity to take action will be. Every action will have a result. Every inaction will leave us to the forces and actions of others or nature, which are not always kind.

So what does physical integrity look like? Like everything else in life, it comes down to visualizing, believing, and doing. I used to pray that I could know, then that I could believe, then that I could do, and finally that I could be. The process is knowledge, belief, action and results. Like most sandwiches, the meat is in the middle—belief and action. If we want to "be" in shape, we must follow the process.

What keeps us from taking action?

False Beliefs

We choose what we want to believe. This is the most powerful concept in personal development. It is as easy to choose to believe one thing as it is another thing. If we choose to believe that we cannot do something, we cannot do it. If we choose to believe that we can do something, we have taken the first step toward getting the result we envision. There are more steps, but that is the first step. We must gain knowledge of what series of actions will result in achieving the consequence we desire and then, most importantly, we must take consistent action in accordance with what we have learned. If those actions do not get the result, we must go back to re-examine the knowledge of what series of actions will result in the consequence we desire to see what we missed. Then we must consistently take the actions again until we get the desired results. It begins with a vision and a belief that correct principles and corresponding action can get the results that we want.

If we choose to believe in false principles and are afraid to give up our false beliefs, our actions (which will be in accordance with those principles and belief) will never get the results we want. Many of us continue to take actions in accordance with false beliefs. Why?

Rationalizations, Blame and Excuses

People often do not want to take responsibility. In order to avoid the responsibility they resort to one or more of the following:

Rationalization

To rationalize is to ascribe an outcome to causes that superficially seem reasonable and valid, but actually are unrelated to the true and actual causes. In other words, when we get a bad outcome physically, we do not want to ascribe it to our failure to take action in accordance with true principles (i.e. eat right and exercise more), so we ascribe it to something like low metabolism, a cause that sounds credible, but for most of us is unrelated to our outcomes.

Blame

Whenever we hear blame, someone is trying to avoid taking responsibility for their outcomes. Blame, by definition, takes the responsibility for an outcome and places it on someone or something else. The dangerous thing about blame is that it has the impact of damming our growth. It sounds so credible. We tell ourselves, "Of course, I would have taken the appropriate actions and achieved the intended result, except for the fact that it was removed from my control by someone or something." Playing the blame game assumes we have no responsibility, and there is no need to look further. You may not even try, if you believe achieving the result is out of your control. Blame is never acceptable. When we blame someone or something else for a poor outcome, we are trying to avoid responsibility. Our willingness to place blame will eventually keep us from progressing.

We should always be willing to go back to the situation and ask, "What could I have done differently to achieve a better outcome? What can I do next time?"

Then we can honestly declare, "I am willing to be the cause of a successful outcome and will adjust my actions to discover and act in accordance with correct principles. If something is not working, I will not continue doing it! Instead I will change my actions and try another approach to get to a successful outcome. I *will* be responsible."

Excuses

Excuses are never acceptable, and are time wasters on the path to achieving positive outcomes. People offer excuses in order to avoid blame. Rather than focusing on what role they played, what actions they took, or what actions they should have taken, they seek to be excused for not taking the appropriate actions to achieve the desired outcome.

Another reason we avoid taking correct actions and continue to take actions that do not lead to the desired result is that we are unwilling to eliminate conflicting actions out of our lives. We want to diet and lose weight, but we are unwilling to reduce our serving sizes, or at least change the way we eat. As long as we are unwilling to compromise or sacrifice conflicting actions, we will continue to achieve the results that we do not want. Another insight gained from Winn Claybaugh, author of *Be Nice or Else!,* was that he was willing to give up violent movies and television in order to develop his ability to be nice. He was willing to give up late night socializing in order to get the amount of sleep he required to achieve his outcome of being nice. He was willing to eliminate other actions from his daily schedule, so that he could schedule time to be nice.

It is the same with physical integrity. If we desire to be healthy, strong, and capable, we must avoid rationalizations. Instead we should find out what works, eliminate conflicting practices, and substitute correct principles which we consistently follow. These steps lead to taking action in accordance with true and correct principles that work.

In this regard, affirmations of correct principles probably have more impact than the large decisions. Traditionally, on January 1st many of us resolve what we are going to do during the ensuing new year to achieve a desired result. One big decision is not as important in achieving the result as many small daily decisions we make every minute day after day. Those are the important decisions and the better we get at making them, the more consistent our actions will be.

Social scientists tell us that one has to take an action ninety (90) consecutive times before it becomes a habit. Once a person develops a habit, the action becomes easy and that person will consistently achieve the outcome they are looking for. Most of us are pretty good at making the big decisions, but not as effective at consistently making the small daily decisions. As we make small decisions and act on them, making and acting on them will become second nature. Our focus, then, should zoom in on making and taking action on small decisions in accordance with correct principles consistently without excuses, blame or rationalization!

CHAPTER 17

BUILDING FINANCIAL CAPACITY

"Do what successful people do."

-George Brunt, Idaho Pioneer

Financial capacity is built in the same way as the other capacities discussed in this book. It is taking action on a daily and consistent basis in accordance with the laws of financial management. One advantage here is that the laws are fairly well identified. Here are a few:

> **Pay yourself first.** Of every dollar you make, you will only get to keep a very small percentage. The greater part of an earned dollar is already spoken for in advance by the government, mortgage

231

lender, vehicle payment, utilities, etc. People who are financially successful remember to always and consistently pay themselves first. They might only take ten cents or three cents from every dollar and pay it into a savings account, but they do pay themselves first.

Make more than you spend. This is a basic law of financial success. It could also be looked at as spending less than you make. Either way, there is a series of actions you must consistently take to achieve this result.

Work is the essential element. There is no get rich quick scheme that can give lasting financial success. If you are unwilling to work—that is to take massive and consistent action or effort to produce or accomplish something–you will not create much value at all with your allocation of time. Work is a virtue worth pursuing as its own reward. People who have set the personal goal of finally getting to the point in their lives where they are no longer required to work have misplaced values. Work is an eternal law and true principle. It is a privilege to be able to work, since the result of work is to produce or provide something of value to ourselves or to others. Work is a fundamental law of financial capacity.

Create value for other people. Another very important law of financial capacity states the value created for other people is the sought- after outcome. It is not the money. Money is merely a symbol to recognize and store value. The people with the greatest financial capacity are the people who have been willing to take actions to be the cause of producing and creating the most value for the largest number of people. The many people who have been blessed by their efforts are willing to show their appreciation by conferring value (or money) to the one who took the actions to create the value for them. There are even higher measures of value than money such as respect, honor, appreciation, and love. Too many people want to make money, but not enough people want to work or take action to create value for other people. Money is one way of keeping score of the value you render to other people vs. the value they render to you.

People who have great financial capacity keep the score and do more. While they measure their score in terms of dollars, the reason they keep score is to measure and improve the value of their services. If other people are rendering more value to them than they are delivering through their actions to other people, they increase their own actions to provide more value, and are careful to decrease their indulgence in the values created by others. There is a balance.

Accountants call the score card a balance sheet. Anyone with significant financial capacity has one and can tell you the score without looking. (At any point I can tell you my net worth within a few thousand dollars.) Net worth is a statement reflected in dollars that keeps score between the value you have rendered to others over your lifetime vs. the value others have rendered to you. The goal is to keep that balance positive, but it requires daily consistent action or work.

A profit and loss or income statement is a similar device for keeping track of the value balance you are delivering or consuming during a specific period of time. It is an early warning that you need to dial up work or dial down consumption. High capacity people use a budget to project the value balance to dial up their efforts or dial down their consumption to keep the out flowing value higher than the value being consumed.

A key principle in developing your financial capacity is to remember it is not just the effort that counts—it is the action you take in accordance with correct principles to create the highest value for others. A close friend of mine developed and owned several miniature golf courses and amusement centers. When I visited sites, I often noticed people digging trenches and doing hard labor. Even though these people were working very hard and demonstrating a great work ethic, the value they were delivering was not of high value to a large group of people.The market for these laborers, therefore, confers a relative value that is smaller compared to the person who risked his fortune to build the amusement park for many people to enjoy.

A car dealer named Cal Worthington in Los Angeles coined a phrase, "Sell to the masses; eat with the classes." This is another way of saying that if you deliver the most value to the largest number of people, the universe will reward you with love, respect, honor, and yes, money. Therefore as you seek to build your financial capacity, consider carefully what value you can bring to the greatest number of people. Try to deliver much more than you consume, and you will find yourself in a higher financial capacity position.

The first step for developing more financial capacity is to envision yourself delivering a specific value to many people. What does that look like? What value are you giving? How is that changing or improving the lives of other people? How do they feel about you? What do they say to you in conversation, letters, and emails? How does that make you feel? Create some affirmations that place you in the situation of delivering high value to the most people. Believe that you have something to offer. Belief is actually a prerequisite for taking the first step of envisioning.

Next, observe other people who are delivering high value to the masses. What are they doing? What are they thinking? What laws or correct principles are they following for their results? Once you know these things about others, you can duplicate their success by taking the same actions.

Finally . . . prepare yourself and take action. Consistently mirror the actions of financially successful people. Persist and you will achieve similar results.

CHAPTER 18

ACHIEVING BALANCE

**"Life is like riding a bicycle.
To keep your balance
you must keep moving"**

-Albert Einstein

Our lives are interconnected in so many ways we do not fully understand. If we lack integrity in any of the critical areas, we will limit our capacity. It is therefore crucial to develop our capacity in a balanced way in our physical being, our social being, our spiritual being, our emotional being, and our intellectual being. Life is not about *income;* it's about *become.*

Let's explore the ways high capacity versus low capacity in any of these areas can impact the others.

Physical Capacity:

Without physical capacity, how can we have the energy and the stamina to take action? Our physical body is the essential means by which we take actions. Actions have consequences. Knowledge has no consequence, unless put into practice by physical action. Wisdom is of no value unless it influences behavior. We cannot be social without taking physical action. Our feelings and emotions have no consequence unless they influence our actions. Spiritual natures are manifest in physical actions. Everything is connected. One of the primary definitions of integrity is to be whole or complete. We cannot be complete without having high integrity in each of these areas of life.

Social Capacity:

Social interaction is essential to our well being. We first learn and practice social skills in family units. Children learn to converse, share, follow directions, question, and develop manners in the home. These are all social skills they practice as they gain experience and knowledge. Without social skills a child will have difficulty developing intellectually, emotionally, or in other areas of life. They will have difficulty meeting the challenges at school, on teams, in their marriage, and at work.

Emotional Capacity:

Low emotional capacity prevents us from coping with many everyday challenges. We cannot develop intellectually if we cannot face criticism. We cannot develop and grow socially, if we do not have the emotional capacity to look beyond our own needs and wants to recognize and serve the needs of others.

People who have low emotional capacity cannot be coached. They take coaching as a personal attack and retreat into apathy. If you cannot be coached, even in the most basic way, marriage, finances, physical health, and development all become stunted. If you have difficulty accepting criticism at an emotional level, it will be very difficult for anyone to help you identify the laws you are not living or the actions that you must take to achieve your intended results. People are often blind to their shortcomings. We all need coaching. Coaching requires overcoming emotional immaturity. Low emotional capacity prevents us from taking action because our challenges tend to overwhelm us. If you find yourself frequently saying "I feel overwhelmed," work on developing your emotional capacity to deal with challenges. Challenges will always come and we need to develop the emotional capacity to cope with them.

Intellectual Capacity:

If we do not develop the capacity to meet our challenges intellectually we will find ourselves worried, angry and frustrated. In order to develop socially, emotionally, physically, spiritually, and financially we need to know and have experience in studying, asking relevant questions, conducting experiments, reading profusely, challenging yourself mentally, and thinking rationally.

Spiritual Capacity:

Spiritual capacity is the ability to look beyond ourselves. A person who is starving and unable to meet their physical needs cannot look far beyond their own challenges. To develop a deep spiritual nature or the capacity to meet the greater challenges of our existence, we must first have social, emotional, intellectual, financial and physical capacity. When we have high spiritual capacity we are in the "zone". We are focused on the task 100% and not on ourselves, our wants, desires and needs. We are much more likely to succeed in taking action to develop intellectual, financial, physical, social, or emotional capacity when we are focused on the task, the purpose, and others than when we constantly bring focus back to ourselves.

Physical Capacity:

The development of capacity in any of the foregoing areas depends on your ability to take action. Action is a physical manifestation of knowledge and experience. To develop social, emotional, intellectual, financial, or spiritual capacity, you must take physical action. If you do not have the physical capacity to take action, you may feel frustrated and angry, but physical capacity is not about being muscular or having all of your physical faculties. Some of the most engaged people I know are confined to wheel chairs, have lost the use of limbs, vision or hearing.

Stephen R. Covey, the author of *Seven Habits of Highly Effective People*[41] suggests that private victories precede public victories. First, we must realize that we are in charge of our own development, that we have the ability to be proactive, and that we can choose our own response to any stimulus. Second, we must begin with the end in mind, or decide what it is that we want

---

[41] 7 Habits Summary: (1) Be Proactive (2) Begin with the end in mind (3) Put first things first (4) Think Win-Win (5) Seek first to understand, then to be understood (6) Synergize (teamwork) (7) Sharpen the Saw (Seek balance and renewal).

and why, where we want to go, and what we want to be. Thirdly, we must prioritize our actions putting the first things first, and organize our activities within our allotted time. By doing this we take charge of our own development; we become what we want to be. Stephen R. Covey is a personal friend and has been an enormous influence in my own life. It was his influence and urging that brought about this book. Dr. Covey explained well how we can develop and take charge of our personal destinies along with resultant personal consequences, and build upon those to obtain public victories and synergies. However, I have known many devoted followers who were enthusiastic about the ideas, but never, or for any extended length of time, actually put the Covey's seven habits into practice. Knowledge of the ideas seemed enough for them, but they were not making the connection between their actions and their capacity. They were taught but did not do, so they remained at the same level of capacity they were at previously, thinking increased knowledge of what to do was enough.

The wisdom of the Bible says; "therefore to him that knoweth to do good, and doeth it not; to him it is sin."[42] Why would this be sin? It does not result in the development of capacity. Our growth is stopped and we are "dammed" in a literal sense. It is especially tragic when we know what to do. Only taking action in accordance with correct principles has a consequence. Knowledge and thinking only have impact as they inspire us to take an action. Integrity is the quality of putting knowledge into action. As we take action, that action becomes easier to take, and we find ourselves in a cycle of growth and development in each of the areas of our lives. Our physical capacity will contribute to our emotional capacity, our emotional capacity will contribute to our social capacity, our social capacity will contribute to our financial capacity, and our spiritual capacity will contribute to each of the other areas.

---

[42] James 4:17 King James version.

It therefore is vital for one to develop a method to take daily actions in each of the areas of life. Interestingly, all of the high capacity people interviewed for this book use a planner to plan their actions, and to be certain they devote some amount of time to taking action in each of the areas of development that we have discussed. Their daily action lists would include things like reading scripture for 30 minutes a day, devoting one out of ten hours each day to a charitable action, working out at the gym with friends, accomplishing two items on their written plan, dinner with their spouse or family, and reading a quality book for 30 minutes. In every case, we found action items addressing spiritual, emotional, marital, financial, physical, and social goals. Even actions like going to bed at a certain time were prevalent. Rest is a weapon! It has been shown to enhance intellectual, physical, and emotional performance.

Organizing our time and planning ahead to take action is essential to actually taking action and achieving higher capacity. It does not happen by chance. Balance happens on purpose.

W. Clement Stone advised, "Have the courage to say no. Have the courage to face the truth. Do the right thing because it is right. These are the magic keys to living your life with integrity."

Mihaly Csikszentmihalyi, Hungarian psychology professor and author, spent years of his life searching for what makes a life worth living. What is it that makes us happy? The results of his studies are extremely interesting and enlightening. He theorizes that we are happiest when we are both highly challenged and have the capacity to meet the challenge. It is then we can be in a state of "flow," or complete absorption with the activity or situation at hand. If we lack the spiritual, emotional, intellectual, financial, social, or physical capacity to meet our challenges, we cannot be in a state of happiness.

Capacity Versus Challenge Chart 1

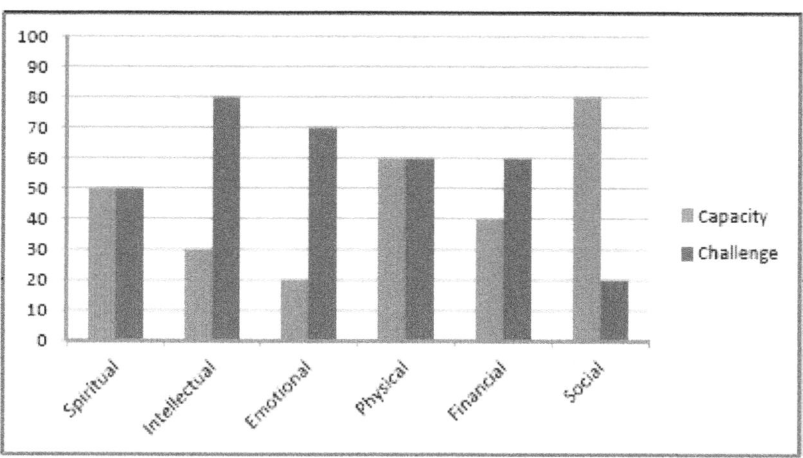

The person depicted in the above chart is neither happy nor successful. With a median score of 50% for spiritual challenge and a corresponding capacity he is satisfied, but not engaged spiritually. Mihaly's studies have shown that a person must be challenged above the median to enter "flow." He is frustrated intellectually because his capacity is not high enough to meet his challenges. He has high anxiety and fear emotionally, because he is adequately challenged but does not have the emotional capacity to meet the challenge. He is "in the zone" physically and feels good about himself because he is challenged above the median level and has the capacity to meet the challenge. He has anxiety financially because his capacity is below his level of challenge, and is bored socially, where his capacity far exceeds his level of challenge.

Capacity Versus Challenge Chart 2

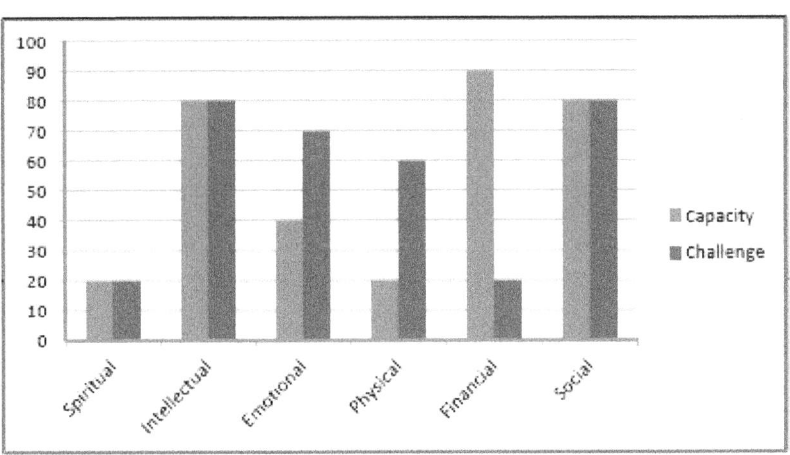

The person depicted above is still not happy even though she has the capacity to meet heavy challenges intellectually and socially where she has both significant challenge and skill.   She is still not happy or feeling successful because she is experiencing apathy spiritually, and is ignoring that aspect of her development. She is emotionally over-whelmed because her challenges far outweigh her skill and capacity to deal with her challenges. She is frustrated physically because she does not have the capacity and stamina to meet her challenges. She is bored financially because she has lots of capacity but few challenges and feels undervalued.

Capacity Versus Challenge Chart 3

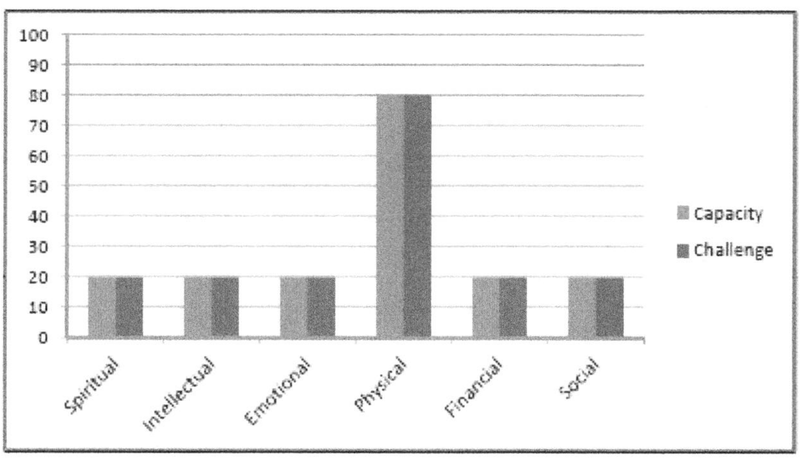

The person depicted above is not happy or successful, because even though he has full capacity to meet all of his challenges, his challenges are not sufficient to engage him. People cannot be happy in the absence of opposition. Few people are without challenges. There must be a certain level, a medium point of challenge before we can be happy. When the challenge is low we spend our time in worry, apathy, relaxation, or boredom. A person in this situation must challenge himself and develop the capacity to overcome those challenges in order to be happy.

Capacity Versus Challenge Chart 4

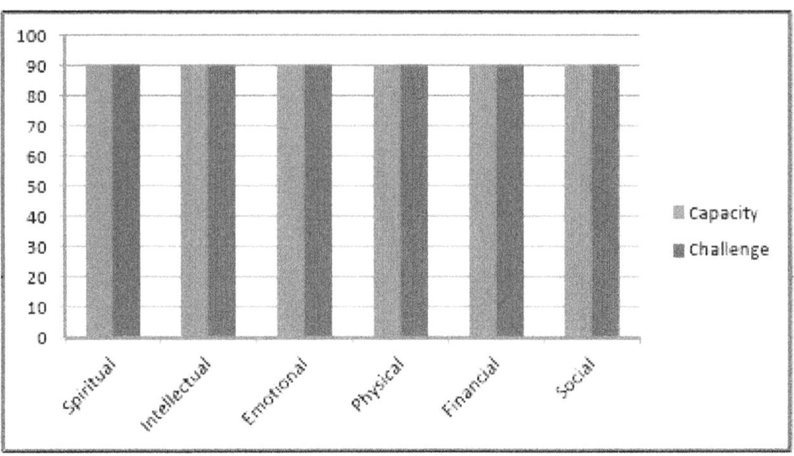

When we are highly challenged and have the capacity to meet our challenges we are in a different state of being. This state of being is characterized as euphoric. It is becoming so focused and involved that we become selfless. It is like the concert pianist performing a difficult piece with perfection. Some have described that experience as being so in tune that nothing existed outside of the performance–a time of total outward focus.

Several studies have shown that only about 20-30% of people rate themselves as happy, even when their median income, adjusted for inflation, nearly triples. Most people do not feel happy, because there is an imbalance between capacity and challenge in one of these areas of life. They do not realize that they can move from apathy or boredom by increasing their capacity. Many challenges will always be there as they are a regular component of life. We can also challenge ourselves. When we do not take action to increase capacity, we are choosing apathy and boredom.

We increase our capacity by increasing our integrity. We increase our integrity by facing the truth (the laws that govern systems), and always acting in accordance with those laws. We systematically get results and learn (knowledge) how to get more results (experience) and thus increase our capacity.

The sub-title for this book is *Build Your Capacity for Success and Happiness.* If you have read the book to this point, Congratulations!" How are you doing in assimilating the information and its meaning? Are you ready to take the necessary actions to become a person of even more capacity?

The final key is:

**To be happy,
focus on building your capacity
to match your challenges
and make sure
you are sufficiently challenged.**

Take daily action to achieve the positive consequences you want in your life. You will gain experience and knowledge, the two main components of capacity. Discover new challenging systems and master them. This is the process of integrity which is the key to capacity! It is the key to happiness and security. Happiness is having the capacity to handle the difficult challenges that come to us. That is how we move toward being complete, integral, and whole.

Sometimes we seek a life with minimal challenges. This path leads to apathy, worry, fear, anxiety and inaction. Only actions have consequences. People with the hope, courage and faith to take daily actions to increase their capacity enjoy security, success and happiness.

May you, your organization, your marriage, your family, your daily life be filled with integrity, the key to capacity. If you continue in the course, your confidence and abilities to obtain what you truly want will increase as you progress toward the day of having perfect integrity and unlimited capacity.

APPENDIX A

ANSWERS TO AD SLOGANS

1	· · · · · · · · · · · · ·	ACE Hardware
2	· · · · · · · · · · · · ·	Alka Seltzer
3	· · · · · · · · · · · · ·	Allstate
4	· · · · · · · · · · · · ·	American Express
5	· · · · · · · · · · · · ·	AT & T
6	· · · · · · · · · · · · ·	Budweiser
7	· · · · · · · · · · · · ·	Burger King
8	· · · · · · · · · · · · ·	Campbell's Soup
9	· · · · · · · · · · · · ·	Charmin
10	· · · · · · · · · · · · ·	Coca-Cola
11	· · · · · · · · · · · · ·	Dial
12	· · · · · · · · · · · · ·	Double-Mint gum
13	· · · · · · · · · · · · ·	Energizer Batteries
14	· · · · · · · · · · · · ·	Federal Express
15	· · · · · · · · · · · · ·	Florida Citrus Commission
16	· · · · · · · · · · · · ·	General Electric
17	· · · · · · · · · · · · ·	Green Giant
18	· · · · · · · · · · · · ·	Johnson's Baby Shampoo
19	· · · · · · · · · · · · ·	Kellogg's Rice Krispies
20	· · · · · · · · · · · · ·	Kentucky Fried Chicken

APPENDIX B

FINDING THE PATH TO WISDOM

**Integrity is the framework;
capacity is the door,
but action is the key.**

There are many roads to success. Most of these roads are toll roads and the price you have to pay to reach your destination many times dampens the joy of the success you meet at journey's end. The true road to success is one which allows you to meet your goals and achieve your aims without overwhelming regrets. Hindsight shows you all the detours you could have taken to avoid these many pit falls, but foresight allows you to find the highway that is straight and true. Foresight comes with wisdom. Integrity is the gps (map) but until you apply the action of actually turning the key, and increasing your capacity, can you begin the journey to true success.

APPENDIX C

TWENTY KEYS TO
LEADING WITH INTEGRITY

Integrity is the key.

Integrity is the voluntary
assumption of the law.

The key to increasing capacity is to increase integrity.
Integrity is the honest incorporation
of correct principles
into your life.

Integrity is not merely
"being true to what you believe"
Rather it is "believing and doing
what is true."

In order to have
integrity,
by definition,
one must be able to
understand and
see correct
principles.

**We can increase our capacity by
shrinking the difference between
our intentions and our actions
and by rationalizing less
when we don't accomplish
our intentions.**

**Increased Integrity x Constancy =
Increased Capacity
which produces Increased Security**

**Fears are rationalizations
that can be overcome
by integrity.**

**Developing increased
personal capacity
can be achieved by the
integration
of correct principles
into our lives.**

**Without action,
nothing happens.**

**There is one grand key
to achieving happiness
in our lives.
The key is charity.**

**Love is life's most important
correct principle.**

**Integrity creates an
environment of respect.**

**You have integrity,
if you make and keep
commitments to yourself.**

**We are not defined by
what we possess,
but by what we process.**

Self-denial is the practice of resisting something of value in exchange for something of greater value.

Acting upon correct and true principles always leads to positive results.

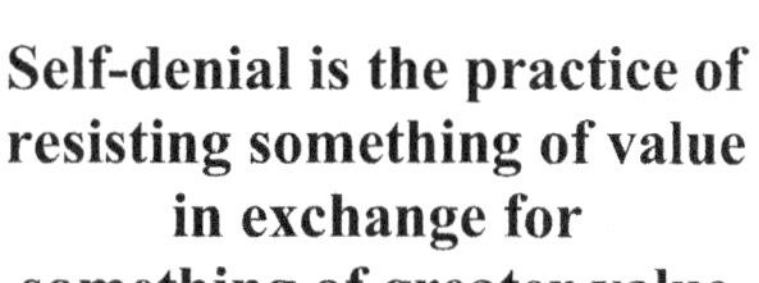

Integrity is the framework; capacity is the door, but action is the key.

The integrity standard for marriage is complete fidelity

To be happy, focus on building your capacity to match your challenges and make sure you are sufficiently challenged.

About the Author

George Brunt is a person of high capacity. He received his Bachelors of Science at Brigham Young University and his Juris Doctorate degree from Pepperdine University School of Law. Currently, he is Chairman and CEO of Byron Union Oil Company, CEO of BiologiQ, Chief Legal Officer at Prosper Holdings, Inc. and runs both a legal practice and a management consulting practice. Over his 34 year professional career, he has served as Senior or Executive Vice President for the following companies: Alcatel USA, DSC Communications Corporation, Quotron Systems, Inc., ITT Information Systems and Qume

Corporation. He is also the founder of Controldocs, Inc., a legal document company and PBW LLC, an owner and operator of premium brand cosmetology schools.

George and his wife, Leslie, recently celebrated their 37th wedding anniversary. They have five married children and seven grandchildren. In addition to the foregoing, he finds time for meaningful service in his church and community, serving or having served on the Advisory Boards of the Marriott School of Business, the J. Reuben Clark Law School, Pepperdine University School of Law, Brigham Young University Idaho, and the Circle Ten Council of the Boy Scouts of America.

If you are interested in further training regarding the content of *Leading With Integrity,* please refer to the resources below:

(1) **The Integrity Coaching Program**, developed by the author, provides assistance to anyone who wants to develop greater capacity in their personal lives or in their organization. Explore the integrity coaching program further at *www.georgebrunt.com.*

(2) The author, George Brunt, can be contacted directly for scheduling individual, small group, corporate, and community training seminars at *info@georgebrunt.com.*

Made in the USA
Monee, IL
28 February 2022

92016505R10148